The Uses of Schooling

Philosophy of Education Research Library

Series editors: V.A. Howard and Israel Scheffler
Co-Directors, Philosophy of Education Research
Center, Harvard University

The recent decades have witnessed a decline of philosophical thinking about education. Practioners and the public alike have increasingly turned rather to psychology, to social science, and to technology in search of basic knowledge and direction. However, while distinctively philosophical discourse has lost currency, philosophical problems continue to surface at the center of educational concerns, confronting educators and citizens as well with inescapable questions of value, meaning, purpose, and justification.

It is the aim of PERL to address such questions through a series of books by new as well as established authors. It is hoped that the series will not only illuminate the philosophical bases of educational practice, but also stimulate the redevelopment of philosophical modes of thinking concerning education. To this end, PERL will publish works of original scholarship in the philosophy of education—encompassing theory, research, analysis, criticism, and interpretation—dealing with all aspects of the educational experience. These works should be of interest not only to philosophers but also to teachers, administrators and researchers in every branch of educational studies, and to the reflective public as well.

The Uses of Schooling

Harry S. Broudy

ROUTLEDGE
NEW YORK AND LONDON

First published in 1988 by
Routledge
in association with Methuen Inc.
29 West 35th Street, New York, NY 10001

Published in Great Britain by
Routledge
11 New Fetter Lane, London EC4P 4EE

Set in Times 10/11pt
by Witwell Ltd, Liverpool
and printed in Great Britain
by Billing & Sons Ltd
Worcester

Library of Congress Cataloging in Publication Data

Broudy, Harry S.
    The Uses of Schooling/Harry S. Broudy.
    P.   CM. — (Philosophy of Education Research Library)
    Bibliography: P.
    includes Index.
    ISBN 0-415-00176-5
    1. Education—United States—Philosophy.   2. Education—United
States—Aims and Objectives.   I. Title.   II. Series.
LB885.B76U84   1988   87–15753
370′.973—DC19   CIP

British Library CIP Data also available
ISBN 0-415-00176-5

To my teachers, colleagues, and students

Contents

Acknowledgments

If the reader detects a tension between a version of classical realism and Kierkegaardian existentialism in this volume, it is because much of my work in philosophy was an attempt to cope with the difference between the metaphysically and existentially "human". The reader will note the difficulty of combining the concepts and languages of several disciplines, and of satisfying their scholarly expectations.

I hesitate even to attempt acknowledgment of my debt to those whose writings and teaching helped form my own "allusionary base" in the last fifty years. My attempts to formulate the philosophical foundations of education owe much to my teachers at MIT, Edgar S. Brightman at Boston University, John Wild, C. I. Lewis, Alfred N. Whitehead, Ralph Barton Perry, William E. Hocking, David Prall, H. A. Wolfson, and others at Harvard. However, most of my professional career has been spent in examining educational theory and practice, an enterprise in which I owe more than I can catalogue to my colleagues in the Philosophy of Education Society, and a host of school administrators, teachers, and doctoral students. I am especially grateful to the Harvard Philosophy of Education Research Center for an opportunity to contribute a volume to its series.

The author and publishers are grateful for permission to reproduce copyrighted materials to *Tradition and Discovery, the Polanyi Society Periodical*, vol. 12, no. 2, 1984–5, 22–8, the Spencer Foundation for excerpts from my report on Case Studies, and to the Getty Center for Education in the Arts for permission to quote from my monograph, *The Role of Imagery in Learning*; also to Faber & Faber Ltd and Harper & Row Inc. for permission to quote from 'Mushrooms' from *Sylvia Plath: Collected Poems*, edited by Ted Hughes, and to Macmillan Publications for 'Sailing to Byzantium' by W. B. Yeats.

Proper claims and expectations

Another book on the uses of schooling calls for explanation if not justification. There is no lack of books, essays, reports, and editorials deploring the status of schooling, and no dearth of recommendations as to what must be done to save the nation put at risk by illiteracy, the destruction of family values, invasion from alien armies, drugs, pornography, foreign-made automobiles, steel, and textiles.

Living through many waves of educational reform has made me wonder why they occur so frequently—roughly every decade. In the 1930s the schools were allegedly not meeting the exigencies of the Great Depression, and in the 1940s there were complaints about the educational inadequacy for the war effort. In the late 1950s the nation was at risk of falling behind the Russians in space exploration. So in the 1960s the public schools were chided for failure to teach mathematics and science, or to teach it properly. Commissions were organized to reorganize the curricula in these fields, and summer institutes were designed to bring secondary teachers up to speed in them. The new math would make children literate in number theory rather than or as well as competent in computational skills.

By the late 1960s and early 1970s the Vietnam fiasco together with various liberation movements sparked a revolt against fixed curricula and teacher authority at all levels of instruction. The public school was accused of being the arm of an oppressive society. There emerged proposals for alternative schools, campaigns for vouchers to enable parents to choose among them, private schools, schools that promised to preserve the creativity and free development of the child, and schools adapted to the needs of minorities, the poor, and special constituencies. Early childhood education flourished.

At the same time behavioral objectives, return to the basics, and competency-based training of teachers made their bid for attention and funds. The teaching of reading became a major industry. Today the nation is declared at risk because the schools are not preparing pupils for participation in the technology-driven, market-oriented society.

These tides of reform demand that social crises be solved by correcting the *way* schooling is delivered to pupils by its curriculum and teaching staff. But how is their adequacy to be determined? By testing the product, i.e., by measuring the amount of school learning that has been retained in post-school life. Liberals and conservatives expect the school to have provided content and skills that would result in the "correct" preparation for adult life. It follows that failure in life can be traced to the wrong content taught by incompetent teachers. Or does it follow? Why do the reforms of one decade lead to crisis in the next?

For example, some of the reform campaigns are waged under the banner of excellence; others under that of equality. Are both goals compatible? Excellence connotes superiority — intellectual, economic, social, moral — the antithesis of equality. Private and special schools can opt for excellence; can the public school do so? Put somewhat crudely, can we have excellence without snobs and equality without slobs? This question led my colleagues, B. Othanel Smith and Joe R. Burnett, and myself to write *Democracy and Excellence in American Secondary Education* in 1964.

We distinguished excellence as it applies to a curriculum from excellence in achievement. The former can be determined by the quality of the content; the latter depends on the ability of the schools to adjust the teaching of that content to a wide range of learning conditions. The validating authority for the first kind of excellence is the consensus of the learned in the arts and sciences; for the second, a consensus of the learned in educational theory and practice. Given both, excellence and equality need not be reduced to a rhetorical slogan.

But how does one justify a uniform curriculum — general studies — to a wide range of occupations, family, community, and cultural backgrounds? General studies, sometimes called liberal studies or the humanities, are troublesome to justify. On the one hand, they are almost universally respected and established as indispensable to the educated mind; on the other, their usefulness, except for the ornamentation of the life of the upper classes and the careers of schoolmasters, has not always been taken seriously. When we are told that in the United States between 1973 and 1974 and 1983 and 1984 there was a loss in bachelor's degrees in education (58 per cent), foreign languages (50 per cent), English (39 per cent), life sciences (20 per cent), mathematics (39 per cent), philosophy and religion (32 per cent), psychology (23 per cent), and social sciences (38 per cent), there is little doubt about what college students thought of their usefulness.[1]

One college dean attributes the decline in enrollments to the "trivialization" of liberal arts education in the late 1960s and early 1970s.[2] At that time students rebelled against many things — parietal rules, grading systems, and fixed curricula. Experimentation, innovation, and, above all, relevance to the life of free individuals were demanded. Colleges responded with an array of experimental courses, units of instruction, and even special colleges within the university. Many courses were listed as "pass-fail" or dispensed with grades altogether.

Today, however, undergraduates do not abandon the liberal arts because they infringe on their individuality and freedom. They opt for the more lucrative promises of business management programs which gained 75 per cent in enrollment during the decade in question. There was also a 137 per cent gain for communications, 57 per cent for the computer sciences, 77 per cent for engineering, 55 per cent for the health sciences, and 12 per cent for the physical sciences.

The disturbers of the academic peace of earlier decades have been succeeded by young people eager for a vocational usefulness that general studies cannot produce except for teachers of these subjects and publishers of texts for their courses. Nevertheless, the belief that somehow the liberal arts have something uniquely valuable to contribute persists. The university may rush to supply vocational tracks for their graduates, but guilt feelings hover over the academic community, which manifest themselves in periodic but short-lived projects to reinstate them in undergraduate instruction.

One of the tasks of this essay is to explicate this ambiguity toward the general studies. It will argue that schooling is used in at least four ways in post-school life, and that some schooling is used not by recalling the content of the courses studied in school but rather by selective forgetting of that content. Admittedly, an air of paradox hovers over this notion, but if it can be dispelled, we may be able to cope with the ambiguity of our attitudes toward general education.

The replicative use of schooling demonstrates the ability to reinstate what has been studied pretty much as it was originally learned. Valuable and necessary as this use is, most of what was learned for replication is forgotten in post-school life, unless it is constantly used and relearned. As for the applicative use, so much sought after in our time but also in other times, this is confined in their application to a well-defined set of problems. Merely studying the principles in general education will not yield the applicative use. What, then, is left? We shall suggest that there are at least two other uses: the associative and interpretive, and these justify general studies.

Another circumstance also contributed to my interest in the uses of schooling. In 1972–4, the Sloan Foundation funded a project to study the engineering curriculum at the University of Illinois and its relation to the social sciences and the humanities. Each semester a number of the engineering faculty together with a representative faculty from other disciplines met regularly and discussed a target problem: energy. Although the project antedated the energy crisis, most of the problems connected with it were beginning to emerge. I had an opportunity to note how well non-engineering professors could follow the engineers' discussion of the problem. A colleague in philosophy of education and I had little difficulty understanding the issues, the methods of dealing with them, and their general import. We did not do so well with the more technical discussions on the sources of energy, the engineering problems of constructing energy sources, devices, etc. Both of us had been exposed to a good scientific curriculum in our collegiate years, but neither of us would have cared to retake our college exams in our undergraduate courses. Our non-engineering colleagues who did not have such a background found the going rough. Conversely, the engineers, when confronted by moral and social issues connected with the energy problem, tended to have recourse to commonsense rather than to the concepts of sociology or philosophy — unless they had taken courses in these areas in their undergraduate days.

Two observations resulted from this experience. One was that, although most of us could not pass an examination in the physics and chemistry we had taken in college, we could understand the discussion. The other was that we know little about how a member of one academic discipline construes the concepts of another. This seems to us to be a fit epistemological inquiry for all those interested in interdisciplinary studies. Above all, however, it strengthened my conviction that the key to such an inquiry lies in the role of general education.

The task has several dimensions. One is to analyze the way these four uses are developed in schooling; another is to indicate the kind of curriculum in the secondary school that develops all four uses rather than one confined to the replicative one used to measure all schooling. Still another is to formulate a theory that makes plausible the notion that we may learn to use general studies associatively and interpretively by forgetting some of the content studied in learning them during school days. The latter task will utilize Michael Polanyi's notion of "tacit knowing" or "thinking with." However, the arguments will not be persuasive unless there is a way of testing the hypothesis. How can we demonstrate that what cannot now be recalled functions? A number of "experiments" will be described that can be used to become aware of the role general studies plays in the formation of the allusionary base — that storehouse of images, language, concepts, and values which constitutes the educated mind and the educated imagination.

Education has sources in psychology, philosophy, economics, and the several physical sciences. In addition, it has developed its own concepts for discussing problems of teaching, curriculum construction, and administration. The difficulty is to use discourse that does not offend either the educationists or the academics in the several disciplines, yet keeps the logic of educational proposals clear to all concerned, including the citizen who pays for it all. This book attempts to maintain this level of discourse, but it would be surprising if philosophers, aestheticians, psychologists, sociologists, and even educationists did not complain that it overlooks important distinctions, omits key references, and generally lacks the level of technical sophistication that their respective disciplines demand from their own scholars. Nor will the educationists have the patience to wade through pages of distinctions and arguments before getting to the tasks of implementation.

Clearly, if one were determined to satisfy all such expectations and objections, a book on the kinds of knowledge and their uses would never be undertaken, or, if undertaken, never be finished. This volume presupposes an interpretive use of courses in general education that educators, academicians, and the educated citizen can be expected to have. There is a sense, therefore, that this attempt to elucidate the uses of knowledge and schooling will serve as a rough test of these uses for the variety of readers for whom it has been written.

Educational administrators may well raise questions of implementation of the suggested programs. After all, the aim of providing general education for the total school population has never been taken literally or seriously in this country. Teachers may be troubled by the suggested program of studies because it differs in many respects from the standard set of subjects constituting the college preparatory curriculum. For example, the curriculum does not include the study of a foreign language, sternly demanded by most of the education reforms of the 1980s, because there is no agreement on the one or even two languages that everyone should be able to learn or the level to which it should be learned. The distinction between health education and physical exercise will trouble others.

This raises the question as to the function of the school among the several institutions that minister to the needs of society in general, of the young in particular. The curriculum described in this essay argues for the special function of the school as the institution primarily responsible for instruction in general education. Other types of instruction and nurturance it may perform because it may be convenient to do so at the school site, not because it is part of its special function. Vocational education, all sorts of arts and crafts, athletics, hobbies can be provided by a community, if it chooses to do so, but they have only peripheral relevance for general education.

If this effort is successful, it may persuade the reader that, although the results of general studies cannot be measured by tests of replication and application, they can be assessed more or less systematically. It may persuade the reader to consider the role of the arts, or more generally aesthetic experience, in the associative and interpretive uses of schooling. If these expectations are even modestly achieved, it may help us answer Spencer's query as to what knowledge is of the greatest worth.

CHAPTER 1

Criteria for uses of schooling

If there is anything about schooling that goes without saying, it is that what cannot be remembered has not been learned. Much of what has been said on the subject, therefore, concerns ploys and devices to guard against forgetting. Teaching the young leaves little room for fugitive learnings. Teachers, pupils, parents, school administrators, and the public at large play out the drama of testing. And dramatic it is, involving danger of failure, a confrontation between the performer and the task, and the suspense of the final reckoning.

To be sure, not all participants in the drama take it with equal seriousness. Perhaps putative candidates for membership in Mensa are not agitated at test time. However, parents worry if their children do *not* worry about tests. Not to take tests seriously is not to take life seriously.

Forgetting, however, is a normal occurrence, and it is not unusual to forget what once had been remembered on a test, so that one can say, "At one time I passed tests on Shakespeare's plays or identified the capitals of all countries in Europe and Asia, but I doubt that I could do so now." Yet schoolmasters, and perhaps all of us, feel a sense of waste in such memory decay and cannot avoid asking what was the point of learning so much that was destined to be forgotten.

It is no accident, therefore, that the history of pedagogy is largely a chronicle of theory and devices to promote learning of a body of content for long-term retention. As early as 46 BC Cicero listed *memoria*: "to secure it in one's memory," as one of the five tasks in learning the art of speaking and writing. The actual teaching procedure both in the school of the grammarian and in the higher school of the *rhetor* involved memorization of the definitions, classifications, and rules as embodied in text books.[1]

The persistence of rote learning, despite the no less persistent denigration of it, is witness to the importance attributed to long-term retention of schooling. Conditioning theory and research from Pavlov to Skinner gave rote learning scientific status and refined its instrumentation. Surely if salivating dogs and gymnastic pigeons can learn and fixate complicated tasks, the school population can be taught facts and skills for life-long availability by the same method.

Accordingly, teaching stresses repetition of facts, procedures, and interpretations of them as stated in a textbook, and that achievement is measured by end-of-course examinations. Even when the instruction introduced problems that required understanding of principles, examination questions might ask for no more than the reproductions of solutions provided by the "sample" problems in the text.

Achievement is measured by similar testing in higher education as well. Entrance is largely determined by performance on tests of what presumably had been studied in the secondary school, and even though higher education demands much more than rote learning of assigned content, there is an expectation that the facts and formulae of those courses remain on tap for lifetime retrieval. If tests show that a goodly portion of adults are functionally illiterate, the schools are in for trouble, especially if the proportion of such illiteracy is greater than that found in the population of other countries that are in economic competition with our own. Throughout school and life, tests of the perdurance of learning are taken as measures of success of schooling.

Life tests, however, may require more than recollection of school learning. An automotive engineer confronted with a design problem is expected to do more than recite the content of engineering courses, even though such recitations earned good grades in those courses. The practising engineer is expected to *apply* the content of those courses to the difficulties encountered in practice. The engineer is expected to recognize the difficulty as one that certain principles will explain and from which possible solutions can be deduced. Beyond that, experience in laboratories or on the job are expected to provide techniques of solving the problem.

In life, therefore, the engineer, physician, lawyer, plumber or mechanic are tested by both their ability to *replicate* what they have learned formally and to *apply* relevant selections from that instruction to the set of tasks that make up their vocations. The plumber is a craftsperson who has learned the standard tasks and solutions as an apprentice to a master plumber. Drilled in the procedures for correcting a specific set of predicaments in plumbing equipment, he applies the procedure to each instance of that class. There is the class of predicaments that might be labelled "stopped up drains," and if this trouble is recognized as an instance of the class, then the rule of procedure for stopped-up drains is put into practice. If the rule does not work, one for another class of difficulties may be tried, but there is a limit to the plumber's repertoire of procedures. If none works, a higher authority must be invoked, perhaps that of the sanitary engineer.

The plumber uses some of his training replicatively, repeating learnings pretty much as learned. One test of the efficacy of the plumber's training would be to recite the rules for some of the predicaments encountered in practice. Such a test, however, would be inadequate to measure the ability to cope with situations in which the rules did not work. The application of a rule is more replicative than applicative; the higher reaches of application entail understanding of principles and theory that generate hypotheses as to the causes of the difficulty as well as suggestions for coping with them.

What is an adult citizen who had the benefit of a general education in the arts and sciences and passed the requisite courses with average or better grades to do when asked to fix a stopped-up drain or a radio that has ceased to function or to remove stains from a tablecloth? The citizen is likely to cut a sorry figure. He cannot fix the stopped drain because he did not learn or has forgotten the particular skills and rules designed to do so. But, it might be asked, "Did you not study physics of which hydraulics is a topic? Should you not be able to apply the theories learned in those courses to this particular situation?" The answer is likely to be "no." The particular situation together with a lack of familiarity with the necessary tools make it unlikely that good grades in the physics class is a guarantee that one will apply that knowledge to cope with the predicament.

On the common criteria for schooling, our sample citizen has failed because he cannot replicate the necessary skill or apply the relevant principles. Yet these are the common criteria for the effectiveness of schooling, and failure on either is interpreted as a failure in schooling. Hence the common query, "What good did your education do you if you cannot replicate or apply it on demand?"

We are thus confronted with a dilemma. Either the schooling was inadequate or the criteria are wrong. If we accept the first premise, viz., that the education was inadequate, we would have plenty of company among those who deplore general education as a waste of time. And should we embrace the second alternative, we are confronted with the task of showing how and why the criteria are inadequate.

To challenge the generally accepted criteria is the more difficult and risky undertaking. Yet on the success of this effort rests the fate of general or liberal education. Is the effort worth the trouble? The tradition of general/liberal education is class oriented, i.e., designed for the use and enjoyment of leisure, specifically, the leisured class. Aristotle pointed this out centuries ago when he argued that the appropriate time for liberal studies was when the individual was free from the duties of the household and state. This follows, Aristotle argued, because "the first principle of all action is leisure." Although both work and leisure are "required, leisure is better than work," and therefore the issue is what ought we to do when we are free from occupation, i.e., during leisure.

But why is leisure better than work? Because, explains Aristotle, the goal of man is happiness, and happiness connotes pleasure rather than the pain and rigor of toil and striving. This hedonic justification is muted somewhat when Aristotle remarks that not all pleasures are equally good and that "the pleasure of the best man is the best, and springs from the noblest sources." It turns out that the best pleasure is to be derived from intellectual activities.[2] However, modern societies have interpreted this dictum differently, viz., (a) that success in the world of work is the highest goal in life and (b) that leisure is the root of all evil. Whether both theses can be maintained by a society that grants special status to those fortunate enough to make earning a living unnecessary is debatable. Nor is the Aristotelian thesis that freedom from toil is to be sought for a chance to exercise the intellect and thereby achieve the highest happiness convincing to many college undergraduates.

Hence the ambivalence toward general or liberal education in modern societies, i.e., those oriented toward economic and political power. It is the pivot on which the seesaw rotates, for on the one side lingers the Aristotelian notion that human beings are at their best when seeking the highest truth about the nature and destiny of the human species and, on the other, the notion that the highest good is success in achieving status, money, power. Modern youth in modern societies may agree with Aristotle's reasoning that leisure is better than work but not necessarily that it be used for high thinking.

Undergraduates worry lest the time required for the liberal studies interfere with the preparation for the world of work, and their parents in all probability share their concern. At the college and university general or liberal studies are extolled in prefaces to catalogues and at convocations. The student is warned that to postpone them is risky because even in the world of work "understanding" has a market value, and that liberal education is a means — perhaps the sole means — to that understanding. Understanding of man and society is essential to successful corporate management, and doctors and lawyers are enjoined to take courses in ethics. The argument may be persuasive, but the rush of students to the schools of engineering and business and flight from general studies indicates that it is not convincing. It is the applicative potential of schooling that is convincing.

At least two other factors lower the credibility of the humanities and liberal education in general. One is the claim that the study of the humanities — the classical mixture of the arts and sciences — will promote good character that in turn will promote good works in all walks of life, even though work will not be abandoned for leisure. From ancient Rome to modern Germany there is no lack of counter examples; neither Nero nor Goebbels was culturally deprived.

Another factor is the atmosphere of the American university itself. In the name of progress, especially military and economic progress, professors and administrators are eagerly seeking profitable arrangements with industry and the military. No doubt the flood of grants such cooperation generates will help scholarship as well as industry. Nevertheless, this eagerness to put the academy at the service of industry may undermine the claim of the academy to freedom of inquiry limited only by its own rules of intellectual probity.

All of which is not lost on the undergraduate. Nor does it escape the attention of the students that even professors of the humanities are not necessarily interested in liberal/general education. Recognition in one's field does not depend on teaching the young to become more "human" but rather on the approval of the learned in one's field. And that is earned by writing, research, and turning out good graduate students.[3]

Another indicator of the ambiguous attitude of the university to general or liberal education is demonstrated by the alternate bouts of neglecting undergraduate studies in general education and guilt for doing so. Periodically a national movement is launched to revive undergraduate teaching by *distinguished* faculty. After a heady burst of publicity, the distinguished faculty return to more distinguished academic tasks and large survey courses are turned over to younger professors and graduate assistants who, in turn, hope some day to be permitted to spend their time on research and writing.

To return to the dilemma that occasioned the discussion of general or liberal studies: either they are inadequate to produce the results claimed for them or the criteria for their success are mistaken. Clearly the first thesis is difficult, perhaps impossible, to establish. The second, however, does lend itself to critical examination.

Inadequacy of the replicative criterion

It is the contention of this essay that general education is being judged by inappropriate criteria, namely, the replicative and applicative uses of schooling, and thus what can reasonably be expected from such education is misconstrued. Some limitations of the replicative criterion have already been mentioned. To use instruction replicatively requires frequent reinforcement by repetition. The multiplication table, spelling of a fairly large repertory of words, facts in history, science, or geography, standard formulae, and problems in mathematics (the square of a binomial or the equation for solving a quadratic equation) can be overlearned to the point that it is virtually impossible to forget them. The same holds for passages in poetry that have been repeatedly memorized for recitation, the names of famous authors and scientists. Frequent drill plus periodic testing insure long-term retention.

Reading the newspaper, bills, letters, and occasionally a book maintains the reading skills; other frequently encountered situations do the same for the skills of writing and computation, provided, of course, they were mastered in the first place. If mechanical change-makers and calculators decrease the need for individual computation mentally or by writing, these skills may not enjoy this long-term retention. As long as these daily routines remain fairly constant, they use schooling replicatively.

Whether these tasks reinforce learnings in the content subjects is harder to estimate. One would expect that repeated references to place names in the news would reinforce the earlier learnings in geography. The large audiences for radio and television might be expected to extend the replicative uses of some school subjects. Doing crossword puzzles, for example, should have a highly reinforcing influence on language skills. The need to read signs and maps as well as a wide variety of billboards and posters must also function in this way.

This may explain the public's incredulity at being told that illiteracy persists, even abounds, in young people who have had the benefit of schooling. They are shocked to hear this from employers who complain about young employees who cannot spell or write an intelligible letter or report, because so much attention, instruction, and repetition (drill) has traditionally been devoted to insure the "shelf life" of these basic skills. Teaching the "basics" for replicative use is one of the few issues on which the school and public are united. The teaching of reading is not only a school activity but a large-scale industry.

As might be expected, the most consistent replicative use of knowledge occurs in vocational life. Vocations vary in the amount of sheer repetition their tasks require, but in the nature of the case the tasks must remain fairly uniform, and the skills required for their performance are reinforced regularly. Skills learned in school and used on the job also have the advantage of constant repetition so that a large repertoire of replicative uses is built up.

However, vocations vary widely in the particular skills they utilize. Office work demands a fairly high order of language skills, whereas a lathe operator may require a complicated set of finely tuned manual skills. A plumber, electrician, or auto mechanic accumulates a set of manual and symbolic skills peculiar to the tasks of a particular trade, and these are used replicatively.

However, much of what has been studied in literature, science, history, or mathematics is not replicated regularly on or off the job, and tends to fade from memory or become fragmented into bits that may or may not be recalled at will.

Two observations follow from these considerations. One is that the replicative use of schooling is an important outcome; the other that its role in the uses of general education is limited. That the replicative use is important should be evident. It utilizes the primary markers of meaning in all the arts and sciences. Without a large store of such rote learnings, we are in the position of foreigners ignorant of our language and who depend on the dictionary for attempts to speak or understand it. Consider, for example, the person who has at one time studied the 100 number facts, the multiplication table, and the spellings of dozens of common words, but has forgotten many of them. Let us assume that these are retrievable from books when needed or let us assume that one can reconstruct them from a theory of language or mathematics. Would it make sense to rely on these indirect sources instead of the automatic use that overlearning makes possible?

This, of course, explains the school's emphasis on the basics. Employers are not satisfied with diplomas that certify successful grades in reading, writing, spelling, and numeration — they expect replication of the original studies and test performances. The defence of the school that passing end-of-course tests demonstrates that the materials had been learned and the corresponding skills formed is insufficient either for employers or ordinary conduct of life.

A more tenable defence of the school would be the decrease of non-school use of these skills in daily life. There is some plausibility to the argument tha the rapid growth of technologies of com-munication and calculation reduces the need for such skills as mental arithmetic and spelling. Even reading demands are reduced by visual displays accompanied by spoken messages.[4]

Nevertheless, hundreds, perhaps thousands, of items studied in school and on which successful examinations have been passed are not recallable in post-school life. They are not available for replicative use. Among these items would be included much of the content of the very courses required to meet general education requirements. How many who passed College Board examinations a decade ago would care to retake them now? How many who took Latin in high school could pass a high school Latin exam today? *Idiots savants* who can recall certain items with astonishing facility aside, for most of us much of what has been learned by the end-of-course examination criterion is not replicable.

If, on national surveys of adults, poor performance on questions of fact in American history that had been studied not once but in many courses is the rule, what justification is there for the study of

American history? And would not the same query be appropriate for the study of mathematics, chemistry, physics, and literature, let alone the increasing number of social sciences?

Inadequacy of the applicative criterion

The doubts raised about the value of schooling when judged by the replicative use is even more accented on the applicative test. By application is meant a process quite different from the replicative reinstatement of an item pretty much as originally learned. It also differs from the use of a procedural rule that "applies" to a class of situations. If wood in the fireplace refuses to burst into a blaze, a familiar chemical principle will suggest an explanation. Without adequate oxygen, there can be no adequate combustion. This was demonstrated in the familiar high school experiment with glowing splinters inserted into test tubes. The pupil learned the principle not only of combustion but of oxidation in general. Does this understanding solve the predicament of the fireplace? Only if the principle can be translated into a procedure for getting sufficient air to the fuel. Many possibilities present themselves, but if they entail complicated operations involving flues and chimneys, the simplest and perhaps safest procedure is to consult a firm that services fireplaces, or, if available, a chimney sweep. Applicative use of knowledge requires both an understanding of principle and the availability of procedures that can be replicated with skill. It is the distinctive use of schooling by the professional — by the automotive engineer, the lawyer, the physician. Professional training combines acquisition and interpretation of theory with decisions of practice. The mix of theoretical understanding and skillful practice determines the professional or paraprofessional status of an occupation. Para-professionals lack the theoretical sophistication of the professional.

The applicative use of schooling or knowledge is a species of analogical thinking. A new problem is compared to a familiar one that one hopes will suggest a solution for the new problem. Whoever first applied knowledge about the power of an electric current to magnetize a bar of iron within a coil of wire and therefore operate a bell completed the analogy $\frac{hand}{clapper} = \frac{?}{clapper}$ and hit on the notion of using the magnetized bar to activate the clapper, i.e., to act as a hand. The invention of the steam engine, we are told, depended on perceiving the resemblance between the behaviour of steam in a kettle and in a cylinder equipped with a piston.

What would measure the temperature of the air? It might occur to someone that what is needed is a pointer that moves in some correlation with heat. If it occurs to us by a twitch of memory that some liquids expand and contract in relation to heat, it may be the first step toward constructing a thermometer. Advances in theory and the technology provide new resources for analogical thinking. Analogy and necessity are the parents of invention.

Little wonder, therefore, that the applicative use has been regarded as the most important life test of schooling — that it justifies schooling in general and the inclusion of a subject in the curriculum. Schools have operated on the assumption that a large store of facts, rules, and principles learned and overlearned for replication would automatically be used applicatively when situations became problematic. When it was noted that the applications did not occur automatically, exercises in application became part of instruction, i.e., application was to be reduced to replication. Unfortunately, such applicative exercises, carried out on a particular subject matter, e.g., mathematics or chemistry, did not guarantee transfer to problems not practised in the classroom.

One reason for this might be called the principle of cognitive entropy. Just as all forms of physical energy tend to degrade into heat, so all forms of mentation tend to be reduced to replicative repetition. For many situations that need fixing, instating the particular procedure that corrected the situation in the past is the most efficient solution. When a society is ailing, it makes sense to apply familiar remedies. When they fail, the citizen perforce has to resort to theorizing about new possibilities. Lacking the theory, one resorts to the appropriate cadre of professionals.

As with the replicative use of schooling, the applicative use as a criterion for judging general education leads to anomalies that sooner or later culminate in proposals to substitute special education for general studies. While there is a compelling directness about aiming schooling at particular results and not to "waste" time in circuitous journeys through theory, the simplicity may be misleading. The attempts of educational research to identify precise objectives and to state them in behavioral terms are supposed to dispel the hazy goals of general education. If complex tasks could be broken down into small and easily identifiable bits, skills for performing each bit could be perfected to a high degree of reliability and with a minimum of cognitive strain. Rules for procedure could be formulated and results evaluated unambiguously. The method is an application of efficiency principles that were so successful in industry and commerce.

The applicative use of schooling is a poor criterion for general education, because, although characteristic of professional practice, it is so rare in ordinary life. It is not unusual or surprising to find college graduates who passed examinations in physics unable to repair a television set or get a balky automobile running on a frigid morning. Even though they may understand the principle of an internal combustion engine and might even be able to explain it to others, they might not recognize the carburetor or locate the key components of the ignition system. In any event, it is much easier to use the technology of the telephone directory and have the garage send an auto mechanic.

It is not advisable to practise medicine on our own bodies even though we may understand the principles of physiology, and no prudent citizen dares an encounter with the courts without the help of a lawyer. Formal study of theory is a necessary but not sufficient condition of application. To solve problems of the kind mentioned requires a wide and thorough familiarity with the class of phenomena to which the knowledge is relevant. Furthermore, it requires familiarity with available procedures, even though the professional may not always perform them. They may be implemented by para-professionals who may or may not "understand" why they are doing what they are trained to do.

Does inability to apply school learning make it useless to undertake general studies? It would make sense to think so, if applicative use is the sole criterion of the uses to which general education is put. In educational literature it has often been taken for granted that the applicative use of knowledge, like the replicative, justifies the teaching of any subject. It is also the view of the public, of many parents and most employers. The waves of school reform deplore illiteracy, inability to write letters of application, and to construe utility bills. Stern measures are suggested for making pupils, teachers, and the "trainers" (the term is often apt) of teachers become more efficient. Teachers as well as pupils, the reports urge, should be tested periodically on the same skills as are being taught to the pupil. Mathematics and science have a secure place in the roster of useful learnings, because they are necessary for training and employment in many business and industrial enterprises.

However, it is obvious that by many, if not most, of the population the arts and sciences will not be used vocationally. The details of courses taken in high school and college will not be reinforced by constant repetition and use. If the replicative and applicative uses are the sole criteria, then for most of the school population and the population at large they must be judged as an adornment rather than a necessity, what Shakespeare called "caviare to the general." To make the case for general education for the whole school population, it will be necessary to find other uses and to suggest methods of evaluating their results.[5]

The associative use of schooling

School learnings are used in nonschool situations in ways that range from the apparently unconscious to the most deliberately explicit. It was once reported that an experiment had been carried on to determine the effect of reading Greek poetry to an infant on the child's ability to learn Greek poetry later in life. Subliminal advertising on television has come under criticism presumably because it effectively uses stimuli of which the viewer is not aware. It is difficult to speculate on the effects of forgotten learnings on behavior. Some schools of psychiatry have capitalized on "forgotten" learnings and their role in neurotic behavior. Schools have not given much thought to the effects of forgotten learnings, in great part because their efforts are directed to preventing them. Even if they were interested in such inquiries, the methodology for studying them is not at all clear.

Many learnings, while not subliminal or unconscious, nevertheless have an air of the accidental about them. For example, suppose the word "Greek" read in a book or a newspaper arouses the thoughts of Achilles or Homer, and these in turn suggest rubber heels.[6]

When asked to respond to a question or cue, something may be resurrected from previous experience. The laws of association — resemblance, frequency, contiguity, vividness, and satisfaction — purport to explain which previous experience the given cue is more likely to elicit. But these are not logical relations. "Red Square" and "red head" are not related logically. They do not imply each other. Psychologically, however, the use of "red" as a cue to a number of red things is common, as the connection between Achilles and rubber heels is not.

Associative use of what is learned in school is frequent, partly because many students and perhaps some teachers mistake an associative relation for a logical one. For example, if the teacher asks, "Why is the sun hot?" a pupil may reply, "Because it is round and bright." This is not the scientific answer, although it is understandable as an associative use of learning, because the sun *is* round and it *is* bright and it *is* hot.

Many a high school student, and perhaps some college students as well, have passed courses by using learnings associatively in responding to questions on essay examinations. They write everything they can recall that is in some way associated with the question. The answer may contain nothing false and nothing that was not in the text or the lecture and yet be wholly irrelevant to the *point* of the question. If the answer is written in a legible hand and with no gross errors in syntax, the chances are pretty fair that it will receive a passing grade. After all, the answer does show that the student was acquainted with the content of the course, and it does have a *kind* of relevance to the question.

This may account for the ambivalence of some teachers toward objective tests. They dispel vagueness of response, but, aside from the difficulty of constructing good multiple choice tests, they do not reveal the associative resources the course may have engendered. Or if the wrong choice does depend on associative connections, it is of no interest to the grader of the test. However, students who have made their way through secondary school by eloquent irrelevance on essay examinations may suffer an unpleasant jolt in college courses taught by less tolerant instructors.

Nevertheless, the associative uses of schooling go beyond passing school examinations. A simple experiment will furnish an interesting example. Undergraduate students were asked to write down the first image (not the lexical meaning) of each of ten words with Latin roots. Usually the class included students with two or more years of Latin instruction and about an equal number who had no Latin. Such words as "conspiracy," "transport," "procrastinate" did not always elicit the images of "breathing with" or "breathing together" or "carrying across" or "for tomorrow" from the beneficiaries of Latin studies, but they *never* occured with the non-Latinists.

The point of the exercise, of course, was not to test the knowledge of literal meaning, but rather to detect the effect of Latin study on the images elicited. What practical difference does it make whether the student could or could not invoke the images corresponding to the Latin roots of the words? For the conveyance of meaning, even precise meaning, perhaps the difference is negligible. But for the reading of poetry or any literary materials, the difference may be very significant, if the author expected the words to arouse associations with particular resonances of meaning.[7]

Or take the following passage:

> The authors discuss several variations of the many-possible-
> worlds view. Other universes could have the same laws as ours,
> but entirely different histories depending on different initial
> conditions before the big bang.[8]

This is not poetry, to be sure, but consider the associative materials that the reader must bring to the construal of this passage. "Initial conditions," "universes," "laws," "many possible worlds" are concepts or complexes of concepts, the construal of which requires understanding of theories in cosmology, astronomy, and physics. These understandings, as will be discussed below, are examples of the interpretive uses of knowledge, or, more correctly, scientific interpretive uses. "Big bang," however, is supposed to arouse not only a theory of the birth of the cosmos, but in addition introduces the sensory images of a loud, sudden noise, perhaps as a culmination of a fireworks display. Associative elements accompany all our experience, even the most abstract and abstruse sort. Do they contribute to our knowledge? And, if so, what sort of knowledge?

The interpretive use of schooling

When A interprets x, x is translated. First, it is a translation in language, second, a translation in logical form. Interpretation is the response to a need for meaning when x does not carry its meaning on its face, so to speak. Suppose a great flood inundates a city. Journalists describe the devastation, estimate the number of displaced persons and destroyed homes. Citizens are interviewed on television and asked how they "feel" about the catastrophe and what it "meant" to them. They answer by listing the hardships and loss they have suffered and the prospects for recovery. The authorities in charge of roads and rivers, transportation, water supplies, and power will answer the meaning question by reconstructing causes and effects in terms of the relevant theories. The state's governor will declare the situation a "disaster," a term that combines emotive and legal meanings. Clearly, there as many "languages" of interpretation. Every academic subject is such a "language." An "educated" interpretation employs the appropriate languages.

A common form of interpretation reconstructs the history of an event or a problem. This particular flood is interpreted by recounting previous floods and their consequences. The historical explanation may differ markedly from the engineering one in categories and terminology, but both are interpreting the event by translation.

One type of interpretation, however, is neither scientific nor technical. Even the term "language" is a very special use of it. Here the meaning is conveyed by an image, often, but not always, a work of art. We may call this type of interpretation *aesthetic* in that it conveys human import *via* the senses. Images that convey human import by their very appearance are probably far more frequent and potent than scientific interpretation. One swift glance at a house, its lawns and hedges, the size of the lot conveys a complex of meaning to the passer by, the neighbor, the realtor. The realtor may try to verify the aesthetic interpretation, but others probably will not. For most of us in most departments of ordinary life, appearance, despite warnings to the contrary, is the clue to reality.

The flood as presented by photographs, the sounds of rushing water, the water levels rising to the upper stories of houses all convey meaning directly by invoking associative resources. The meanings are not stated in causal or historical terms; rather they instate feelings about the powers of nature *vis-à-vis* those of humankind.

Appearance as a key to interpretation is subject matter for theories of aesthetics and philosophy of art, as well as the cosmetic and fashion industries. Each culture, one may assume, develops standardized images of its values, and there is little doubt about their efficacy in controlling interpretation. As a rule, one learns the meaning of such images by living in a culture and undergoing the positive and negative reinforcement by one's peers. The home and school contribute their share; vocation and the media are potent influences. The school introduces the pupil to other cultures as revealed by their appearance as well as by the verbal description of textbooks. Art, in literature, music, or painting, creates images to convey human import or values. These messages are not encountered in the ordinary day-to-day transactions in home, office, or even in the media. This raises the question whether the fine arts, the arts that have been subjected to serious study by art historians, aestheticians, and art critics, can and should "educate" interpretation in the same sense that the study of the sciences "educates" the interpretation of physical phenomena. It is a central issue in defining a curriculum for general education or liberal studies.

Experience becomes intelligible only in so far as the mind orders the phenomena. The educated mind orders experience with the resources of the arts and the sciences. While there are informed sources for interpretation — common sense, common knowledge, common images — that may be acquired without tuition, the interpretive use of schooling according to the concepts and judgment of the "learned," is its most distinctive contribution to the individual and society.

Critical thinking is one of the outcomes generally expected from schooling. All citizens are expected to think critically in all departments of life, but especially in those that have societal import. By critical thinking is meant the testing of discourse for truth and validity. "Is this statement true?" "Does it follow from the evidence adduced for it?" The form of critical thinking is provided and regulated by the rules of logic, definition, classification, and inference. However, critical thinking is *about* a content other than logic itself. We must know something about the field in which the "good" thinking is to be "applied." It is this content that enables us to judge the relevance of proposals and their alternatives. Can general education build the knowledge that will be available for educated or enlightened interpretation of the diversity of circumstance that calls for critical thinking?[9]

The allusionary base

The associative resources provided by schooling and experience plus the interpretive repertoire of concepts and images constitute the allusionary base. The resources of the allusionary base are not used by simple replication or application of this or that school learning, and their adequacy cannot be judged by tests of replication or application. On the contrary, the success of general education is to be measured by the depth and quality of the allusionary base.

The allusionary store or base is the key to associative and interpretive uses of knowledge. Explicit statements in any language — even the most abstract — depend for comprehension on the store of concepts, images, facts, and individual history. The visit to the allusionary store may be systematic, precise, and strictly controlled as in scientific discourse, or it may wander through byways or memory according to the laws of association, or, as some would have it, according to the laws of dissociation.

The discussion of the uses of knowledge may give the impression that the applicative use is confined to vocational activities. The term "specialist" is the more appropriate term, because there are amateur connoisseurs who are specialists and who use knowledge applicatively. There is, of course, the figurative claim that education should produce connoisseurs in living. Such a claim, if taken literally, demands specialism in every department of thought and action. Taken more sensibly, however, it connotes the knowledge that the academic disciplines supply to the allusionary base.

An excerpt from a Norman Cousins editorial on the work of Albert Schweitzer (*Saturday Review*, March 16, 1963) described his work as a doctor, philosopher, theologian, social worker. One ten-year-old boy in response to the name of Albert Schweitzer after reading the editorial, gave the following associated items: "missionary," "mustache," and "doctor." "Theologian" was a man "interested in theories" and a philosopher was "you know, a sort of brainy type." The notion of "an indwelling God" baffled him completely.

How was the youngster using schooling? Replicatively, he was using the skills of pronunciation and syntax as well as the visual habits involved in reading. Associatively, his previous learnings were functioning well enough to give sense to most of the sentences. He had enough knowledge to interpret what it was about. Roughly, he could comprehend the idea of a doctor in an African jungle, a learned man who had some difficulties because of his religious beliefs. He had cognitive maps, albeit exceedingly rough ones, on which some of the sentences could be plotted. It would take much more knowledge about Schweitzer, a clearer notion of philosophy and theology, not to mention musicology — the editorial made reference to Schweitzer's career as an organist and organ builder — to "understand" the passage.

However, there is no "problem" to be solved by the reader. He does not need to "apply" his knowledge. He used some of his schooling to interpret the editorial, but clearly his interpretive resources were not ready for the task. A theologian might scrutinize the article for accuracy and cogency, and so might a student of emerging countries. A specialist would apply theoretical knowledge plus practical experience to evaluate the article and perhaps to suggest an alternative analysis. An editor might concentrate on details of literary construction and rhetorical effects.

Schooling adequate for interpretation may not be sufficient for application, while some applicative knowledge may be too narrow for adequate interpretive use. Interpretational use can be made precise by study, but it does not follow that it will automatically shade into application. A philosopher of science can be very precise about the logic of scientific method, but remain baffled by a bubble chamber problem in physics.

For a society in which vocational specialization is central, the differences between specialized and general education is of the first importance both for curriculum construction and the criteria for evaluating it.

CHAPTER 2

General education — proper claims and expectations

In a modern society most of childhood and adolescence is spent in schools; the costs, private and public, are substantial. Little wonder, therefore, that education is expected to yield commensurate rewards in personal success and public virtue. College graduates, by unspoken but common consent, "should know better" than to indulge in lower-class lapses from virtue. Socrates wanted to know why, if virtue can be taught, as Protagoras, the Sophist, claimed, so many eminently virtuous fathers are disappointed by the lack of virtue in their sons. To which Protagoras responded with an explanation that society as a whole is constantly teaching virtue — a thesis that has relieved the philosophy department of the responsibility to do so.[1]

That neither the art nor science of pedagogy has been able to produce the anticipated benefits for large heterogeneous populations prompts the conjecture that the expectations were not formulated properly. Perhaps the question raised by Herbert Spencer, viz., what knowledge is of the most worth? and what pedagogical maneuvers will produce it, lends itself too readily to ambiguity. If we insist on the answer taking into account the range of individual differences, the question might almost as well remain unasked. The public wants a payoff on educational investment in the whole range of values: economic, health, citizenship, recreation, associational, intellectual, moral, religious, aesthetic, i.e., all the ingredients of the "good" life. With the exception of the economic values, it is general education that is supposed to supply the ideational and dispositional resources for their realization.

When the value recipe for success in life is well defined, the school can concoct programs to meet the expectations of its clientele. This occurs when one social class dominates the success routes of the culture. The values of this class, practically speaking, define the good, the true, and the beautiful. Whatever style of schooling this class chooses for its children is *ipso facto* "quality education." The college preparatory curriculum, for example, incorporates selections from the disciplines that traditionally have been prescribed for the educated classes. When, however, the clientele of the public school becomes highly varied and the success routes of the culture greatly differentiated, the public school is forced to try to accommodate the differences. Vocational and business curricula are introduced to supplement the "general" one, both for economic and social reasons. It is argued that such courses will keep youngsters in school and off the streets.

Nevertheless, that college entrance requirements stipulate units in the arts and sciences has kept alive a respect for the "best that has been thought and wrought," the classical ideal. Although "classical" once connoted the highest forms of Greco-Roman art and literature, the term has come to mean any work worthy to serve as a standard or exemplar. The limited time available for formal schooling makes exemplars an attractive strand in the general education curriculum. Study of the classics, it is believed, has high transfer value for a genuinely *human* life, a view to which, Werner Jaeger argued, western man has returned repeatedly in times of trouble.[2] Despite the current impatience with general studies among college undergraduates, there is no outright rejection of them. On the contrary, the college generation accepts Aristotle's dictum that liberal studies are for those who are already liberated from the economic and political demands of life. The liberation, however, comes after economic and social demands have been met, presumably after retirement. The well-to-do retirees, therefore, are the best customers for general education. They have the time and means to undertake such study, and many of them do so. The retiree contingent, moreover, has a unique opportunity to test how well the courses they took in high school and college function in post-school life, especially in the latter years of life.

When, for example, the elderly Mr and Mrs So-and-So enroll in an extension class in English literature, how much of what they studied in high school and college courses in English literature can they recollect? Can they read the text? Where are the gaps? How much of what they studied in their undergraduate years can now be used replicatively? How much interpretively? How much associatively? Do contents — names, places, ideas — come to mind as the course progresses? Do they recall facts or generalizations? Do they remember the name of the instructor or the textbook used in those courses?

The responses to these queries will vary not only with the individual but also with the way the material was taught in their high school and college days. Teaching styles differ. The didactic teacher who in high school literature drilled pupils in names, dates, places, and the evaluations of works of literature as stated in the text may have produced enough overlearning of these details so that even after thirty or forty years they can be recalled. The beneficiaries of a heuristic teacher who spent most of the class time on discussion may not be able to recall the who-what-when-how details but may be able to reinstate the aura of the characters and ideas encountered in the course.[3]

Queries addressed to students still in college reveal some anomalies. Over a number of years, freshmen classes were asked to read a Sunday issue of the *New York Times*, to mark in black those items they could understand, and those they could not, in red. Three and one-half years later the same assignment with the then current issue of the *Times* was administered to the survivors in the same group. Although the number of items marked in black had substantially increased over the three and one-half years of attendance in college, some of the students could not recall the texts or instructors in the courses where they might have acquired the new interests. When asked whether their studies had taught them anything valuable, most responded with mild affirmatives.

Another anomaly bearing on the evaluation of general or liberal studies is the expectations we have of proper professional conduct. Why in a culture dominated by a market economy, where every calling like every product is measured by its monetary value, do we expect the doctor, lawyer, or accountant to have a code of ethics? Do we expect a plumber, a banker, or a merchant to work for nothing or for less than the market permits? Would it make sense for a desperately poor person to expect a storekeeper to provide goods and services *gratis*? Yet much to the discomfort of the professional, the public still likes to believe that the professions have not rid themselves entirely of their quasi-priestly heritage. Are their codes of ethics reminders of an implied covenant by which their intercession to help all who need their expertise is rewarded by special status in the society? And are these vestigial remains of the notion that the recipients of their services can properly repay the professional with gratitude — with gratuities?

These anomalies reflect the difference in modes of being: that of objects and subjects; things and persons; nature and culture — a difference that is continually being threatened and reasserted. It is a difference that nourishes the notion and study of *humanitas*, the essential difference between human beings and other members of the animal kingdom. It is no accident, therefore, that the humanities are concerned, one way or another, with these differentia of being. Nor is it accidental that the humanities or the liberal studies are not primarily learned for replication or application, but rather to furnish an imagic and conceptual store (an allusionary base) *with* which to think and feel.

The root of the human difference is not reason or spirituality. These are themselves derived from a more primitive ability to assign symbols and signs to things. Symbols, of course, need not be linguistic. Shapes and sounds, as well as odors, can represent states of affairs, and it may well be that such sensory symbols antedate those of language. Symbolization is a potential for freedom from facticity, because it enables us to deal with the surrogates of fact. Once symbols are separated from their referents, they can be combined freely, far more freely than we can manipulate the world of fact. Imagination can create unbounded fantasies of unbounded pleasures and horrendous pains. What is first imagined as desirable may in time be envisioned as possible. One can then imagine that some of what is imaginable and possible could and perhaps should be realized. The transformations of feeding into dining, shelter into architecture, copulation into love and romance are all effected by the imagination.

The same may be said for the origin of science, for the notion of logical order is an ideal, an imagined state of affairs that balances cause and effect, action and reaction, freedom and necessity. The arts and the sciences had their beginnings in the flights of imagination and its intermittent perches on reality.

The combining and recombining of images, i.e., the activity of the imagination, therefore, can be regarded as fundamental in a very literal sense to all experience that is *human*. There is one type of symbol, however, that deserves special mention — the aesthetic image.

Aesthetic symbolism

Unlike the manipulation of concepts in theoretical discourse, images of feeling operate by association, by concatenations of sensory stimulation and emotional responses, what Susanne Langer called "presentational" rather than "discursive" symbols.[4] We read, "This is the forest primaeval/The murmuring pines and the hemlocks." Literally, trees don't murmur, yet the image of murmuring by trees of great age conveys an aura of feeling highly complex, yet immediately perceived. It is a species of knowledge, but of feelingful knowledge. This metaphorical use of language, of sound, motion, line, and color is the key to aesthetic experience, and the aesthetic experience as encountered in the arts is the deliberate objectification of images that convey human import. Just as we rely on science and philosophy to refine thought, so the humanities rely on art, especially the exemplars of art, to refine feeling and to extend its range.

Imagination and images are central to the associative uses of knowledge. They underlie the relation between the sound of thunder, a dark sky, and impending storms. We can see how after many experiences with the sounds and sights of storms we come to associate them into a complex of perception and memory so that thunder signifies storm. It "sounds" stormy and threatening and the dark sky "looks" that way. A thunderous burst of applause is not threatening, yet the adjective does convey something of the force of a storm.

The tie between language and imagery in schooling goes back a long way, certainly as far as Comenius, an enlightened forerunner of the common school, but celebrated even more for his *Orbis Pictus*, a textbook that used pictures to expedite learning of Latin vocabulary.[5]

Less attention has been paid to the generalizing potential of imagination whereby a highly complex notion can be apprehended directly through a sensory image. Paintings of the Crucifixion or a Madonna may express the idea of holiness more adequately — certainly more immediately — than theological tracts. How do verbal accounts of the details of the battle compare in conveying its significance with the picture of the raising of the flag at Iwo Jima?

The separability of image from referent grants it an independence that is exploited by all the arts. Film can conjure up images of persons and events that in the film are presented as real and for the nonce are so construed by the viewers. These imaginary characters can be thinking about other characters, meanings, and events. Like a hall of well-placed mirrors, there is no limit to the series of images of images of images, etc. Imagination has no principle of self-limitation.

This independence of reality has given imagination a bad press. It can be anticipatory and revelatory of truth, but also indifferent to it. It required a great feat of imagination for Newton to envision the laws of gravity in the fall of an apple. No less a feat is the notion that all men are created equal. Ideals have their origins in the imagination.

Sensory images are particular objects, yet they can portray the highest abstractions. Classical art tried to render the highest ideals in perceptible form; much modern art tries to express disillusionment with them. Coleridge distinguished imagination from fancy, between the merely reproductive imagination and the genuinely productive one.[6] In fancy or reproductive imagination, elements already in the mind are rearranged in more or less random fashion. Productive imagination creates something new and important. If, as Kant argued, the very possibility of knowledge presupposes an *a priori* intuition of space and time, imagination acquires philosophical significance. Spinoza, however, regarded imagination and the fictions it produced as evidence for the need of reason to set it straight.[7]

The ambiguous relation of image to fact is reflected in what might be called a revised version of the Garden of Eden story. If we suppose that the apple Eve was persuaded to eat was the secret that images or symbols can be separated from their referents and then manipulated independently, we can understand why Adam and Eve were forbidden to eat of it in the first place. Not only did it lead to knowledge of good and evil, which destroyed their primal innocence, but it also put into their minds and hands the power of creating what is to be taken as reality, a power reserved to divinity.

Types of associative use

Association of ideas covers all sorts of connection under varying degrees of control. It ranges from idle play of ideas with a minimum of deliberate control to the highly ordered search for ideas to fill gaps in problem solving. The effects of age and mental disease on memory are also relevant to ability to use the allusionary base. These variations may be sorted roughly into formal and informal uses.

We think, we read, we talk. Our words shape themselves into phrases in accordance with the syntactical rules of the language. If the language is our native one, we are ordinarily aware of neither the rules nor the shaping. Learning a foreign language, we are painfully aware of these rules — of the gap between meaning and expression. Consider the response to hearing colloquialisms such as "Dick is a pain in the neck," or "Easy come, easy go." To grasp the meaning of these locutions requires an association of words and ideas that, taken literally, don't make sense. A foreigner, even if armed with a dictionary, might lack the associative resources to render these sentences sensible. The resources were acquired in the previous experience of a native English speaker, the first instance of which has long ago been forgotten. A round red light on a post means "stop your automobile" even though one would be hard put to recall when that particular connection of red, round, and post occurred. When did we learn to associate the appearance of lawns, shrubs, the shape and size of dwellings with marks of wealth or poverty? Surely we were not born with these associations, any more than we inherited the links between the intonations, word position and inflections of speakers and inferences we draw about them. Why are particular images selected as clues in the first place? If it is because of a resemblance, what is its nature? Association of ideas does not explain it; rather it is the resemblance that instigates the association. Presumably a similarity of *feeling* can be discerned in diverse phenomena (pain caused by a muscle spasm in the neck and the discomfort caused by Dick's behavior.) Locating the feeling (pain) in what is literally not a pain (Dick's behavior) gives the locution its aesthetic quality, i.e., its power to externalize feeling for contemplation.

By contrast, when confronted with a predicament, we search the allusionary store for remedial resources. We try to recall what we did in a previous *contretemps* of the same kind. In some instances the right recollection occurs and the predicament is relieved. "What did I do before in this situation?" is a request for explicit use of associations. If the needed associative item does not recur or does not work, we may run through our repertoire of trial-and-error techniques. If all fail, we must begin to *think* about possible solutions.

Explicit use of associative resources is not quite the same as problem solving proper. Associative uses are always instances of recall and to some extent can be explained psychologically by the laws of association — resemblance, contiguity, frequency, vividness, etc. Problem solving sooner or later has to resort to a theory that helps generate hypotheses, so that predictions can be made and tested, i.e., logical procedures. If the automobile stalls at an intersection, there are a number of possible causes. If by trial and error we exhaust our available list, we must give up or ask by what facts or procedures each possible cause could be tested, e.g., lack of fuel, failure of the ignition system, etc. Associative resources are necessary for problem solving, but not sufficient. Abstraction from the particularity of the problematic situation, recollection of the principles involved, the if-then possibilities to be considered, and verification of the predictions constitute the hypothetico-deductive method characteristic of scientific thinking. However, even systematic thinking is helped and occasionally transformed by a new insight into possible resemblances made possible by the imagic resources of the allusionary store.

Whether Jung's collective unconscious exists may be debatable, but the existence of a communal memory bank, a communal imagic-conceptual store is an unavoidable hypothesis. It contains the values and verities that for the members of the group go without saying (the tacit ground of community) in the form of folk art, gnomic sayings, proverbs, legends. These contents may be shared without formal tuition, but once the allusionary base includes the products of sophisticated arts and sciences, the gateway to sharing is through formal schooling. The rationale for general education depends heavily on the need for such a common allusionary reservoir. That an adult who passed examinations in general studies while in school cannot now recall most of their details or apply their principles to life problems does not prove that the studies were useless. We could not share *educated* discourse if they were.

Schooling as an associational and interpretive resource

If so much of the associative store is supplied by the ordinary encounters of life from early childhood on, what is schooling expected to contribute? What differences would one expect to find between the allusionary base of the schooled and unschooled adult? Could the difference be detected without consulting school records? The replicative use of school is a straightforward reinstatement of particular learnings pretty much as originally learned. Most school instruction probably has the replicative use in mind as a criterion for good schooling and learning. Does what is not replicable become part of the associative store or is it gone forever?

On the answer to this question depends much of the justification of general studies. For example, the person in our hypothetical stalled automobile may have taken courses in physics and chemistry in high school and college. Suppose the courses were satisfactorily completed, i.e., course examinations were negotiated successfully, but many years ago. Today our subject probably could not pass those examinations, even though the questions have a familiar ring. They are no longer capable of being used replicatively. Is it likely that the principles of an internal combustion engine have also vanished beyond recall? Suppose one were to compare the responses of this person with one who had never studied chemistry or physics and whose knowledge of automobiles was no more helpful than his? What sort of test might provide a significant answer to these questions?

In the example of the balky automobile, we posited the possibility that when trial-and-error scanning of associative resources failed, the subject might turn to a version of the hypothetico-deductive maneuvers of problem solving. Will the resources for using this procedure still function, albeit examinations in the relevant sciences cannot now be passed? Should one expect that enough of the theoretical principles are still available for understanding the problem, if not for applying that knowledge to repair the vehicle? What would test the hypothesis that they are still available?

The interpretive use of schooling consists of translating an existential situation — in this instance, a predicament — into a conceptual one. Predicaments do not become problems until translated into concepts relevant to the class of phenomena of which the predicament is an instance. A problem is a predicament trussed up for analysis. When this occurs we can speak of understanding the situation, even if the understanding fails to be implemented by relevant technical procedures. Interpretive uses of schooling are somewhat like siting a house on a lot. To do so requires understanding the relevance of soil quality, the possibility of proper drainage, exposure to the elements, and the possibility of the view from various locations.

Understanding may require recollection of items learned in formal schooling, but not necessarily in all their detail. Maps vary in their degrees of detail; one that would do very well for the tourist might not be adequate for the surveyor or the roadbuilder. That of the roadbuilder would be of little use to the politician planning an election campaign in a congressional district. The evaluation of schooling as general education is closer to the tourist's requirements than to those of the surveyor, roadbuilder, or the politician.

It does not follow, however, that school input must be as generalized as its interpretive use. Generality is not vagueness. Geography instruction may include a wealth of factual detail, but the decisive factor in interpretive uses of geography is the availability of concepts and principles which the details exemplify. Forgetting many of these details may be necessary for the structure to become available for future interpretive use. However, the forgetting must be selective, not random, and this may well depend on the teaching. If the instruction is didactic and tested only by recollection of details acquired during instruction, the emergence of principles for interpretation may not occur.

Schooling, of course, is not the sole source of interpretive schemata. Language — vernacular or literary — is itself a premolder of interpretation. Atoms and electrons, galaxies and solar systems, causes and effects are categories that depend on formal study. However, the following passage also furnishes schemata for interpretation: "The American dream is a song of hope that rings through the night winter air. Vivid, tender music that warms our hearts when the least among us aspire to the greatest things."[8] These metaphors direct us to compare an ideal with a dream, and a dream with a song that rings (like a bell) on cold nights in winter, and all of these with aspiration to the "greatest things." Any language, to serve interpretively, must first be learned as a set of skills to be used replicatively.

The brain processes by which experience is used replicatively, associatively, applicatively, and interpretively are now under the scrutiny of the computer sciences. At the heart of the search for artificial intelligence is the presumed correspondence between computers and brains, between the computer chip and the fundamental unit of consciousness — nerve cells. However, "chips work at nearly the speed of light, responding in billionths of a second. In comparison, nerve cells, or neurons, work at tortoise-like speeds responding in mere thousandths of a second." The animal response is highly complicated, "depending on the ebb and flow of messages running along its hundreds of thousands of arms.... The other [network] is the silicon heart of computers, whose basic units are relatively simple transistors capable of responding only in two ways: on or off."[9]

Research into brain function may one day render the notion of random associations untenable. As the laws of association are translated into computer operations, they will become less mysterious and presumably more integrated with rational processes of interpretation. The same line of research may also clarify the process of selective forgetting by which details previously well learned are "forgotten" but leave their schemata of interpretation more or less intact.

Schooling resources for interpretive use

The school curriculum supposedly lists the subjects that should produce the content for educated interpretation. The curriculum details will be discussed in the following chapters, but it may be prudent, and perhaps necessary, to elucidate the term "educated." Stripped of socially elitist connotations, the term denotes mental activities regulated, cultivated, or guided by the content of the academic disciplines. The opposite of "educated" here is "informal" or "commonsense," i.e., opinions, judgments, and explanations that are "common knowledge." The information comes from newspapers and other widely available media messages, but also from the community culture.

The distinction being drawn does not imply or claim a superior wisdom or character for the educated mind, albeit such claims are made more or less explicitly in the description of liberal studies in the college catalogue. It refers to the language and concepts used in such courses. Educated astronomy is what scholars of astronomy say about celestial phenomena. Current controversy about astronomical theory indicates that the discipline called "astronomy" is not free from debate on certain matters of theory and perhaps even of fact. However, the controversies are themselves carried on within the bounds of the discipline. There is a difference between educated and non-educated disagreements. Astrologers would distinguish their lore or "science" from the casual use of horoscopes by the laity.

Some disciplines like physics or mathematics are reducible to a relatively small number of basic concepts; others, especially the social sciences, are not. In *Economic Literacy for Americans*, the Committee for Economic Development (1961) listed as basic concepts and institutions such items as scarcity, costs, productive resources, division of labor, economic production, savings, investment, capital formation, labor productivity, market, competition, profit and profit incentive, the price and market system monopoly, public utility, corporations, government taxes, international specialization, and dozens more.[10]

By contrast, the PSSC (Physical Science Study Committee) listed the basic ideas to be studied in the "new physics" as space, mass, mass conservation, light, particle and wave theories of light, motion, force, gravitation, conservation of momentum and energy, electrical forces, electromagnetic radiation, and the structure of atoms.

According to Kuhn, "The study of paradigms is what mainly prepares the student for membership in the particular scientific community in which he will later practise."[11] By paradigms he meant such styles of thinking as exemplified by Ptolemaic astronomy, Aristotelian dynamics, and statistical mechanics. The basic concepts of the academic disciplines are the vocabulary and syntax of educated interpretation.

One can also speak of educated feelings as distinguished from untutored, conventional emotional responses. The latter are shaped by the social *milieu* and become the accepted norms of moral, religious, and aesthetic, as well as intellectual, judgment. These values, when subjected to the systematic scrutiny of philosophy, theology, and aesthetics, can expand and refine both the cognitive and emotional dimensions of these value domains. The educated heart may not feel more deeply about love, anger, and sorrow than that of the unschooled laborer, but the differentiation and range of such feelings are supposed to be expanded by study of the fine arts, more presumably than by the popular arts. Passions of every variety are described and exfoliated in a steady flow of novels, film, and television dramas. Keeping the distinction between actual emotional response and the fictive ones is not always easy, and neither is the distinction between love and passion in a Shakespearean drama and in a soap opera. Aestheticians and art critics work hard and steadily to clarify the difference between popular and fine art, and this itself may be the principal difference. Just as commonsense science, economics, and history can be distinguished from the educated versions by the fact that the latter are products of systematic inquiry, so the fine arts are distinguished by the efforts of academics to understand, interpret, and judge them. Here as in the other domains the school is needed only when serious study of a field is desirable. That the school should stand for teaching the educated version is less debatable in the intellectual domain than in the emotional ones.

"Discipline," unfortunately but inevitably, connotes academic rigidity and constraint of creativity. However, what is the point of formal schooling if not to develop ways of thinking and feeling developed by the arts and sciences? As for stifling creativity and freedom, is it not the uneducated creativity and freedom that are the cause for concern? Helen Vendler, reviewing Roland Barthes's *The Rustle of Language* and *The Responsibility of Forms*,[12] notes that this practitioner of untrammeled "aesthetic discourse" had first to appropriate a series of academic laws, e.g., those of Marxism, semiology, anthropology, psychoanalysis, before he could repudiate them.

It would not be too difficult to mount an argument against the ideal of the educated mind as desirable for the total school population, many of whom will be content to use the fruits of the sciences without the labor of studying them. The same can be said with respect to the other values. Their advice is available without the effort of self cultivation. This attitude is reflected in the impatience of college students with general/liberal education requirements that delay their entrance into professional school curricula. Schooling for replicative and applicative uses is not regarded as postponable; schooling for associative and interpretive uses is.

This is why the strategy of promoting the general or liberal studies by honorific terms alone will not be effective in a modern society where the good life depends on early specialization in the vocational market. The argument must demonstrate the necessity as well as the desirability of the refinements that general education promises. One way of bringing this about is to demonstrate the consequences of *not* acquiring the educated resources for the associative and interpretive uses. The case studies to be discussed in the following chapter represent one approach to such an inquiry.

CHAPTER 3

The search for evidence

If the replicative and applicative uses of schooling cannot justify investment in general education, how do the associative and/or the interpretive uses do so? Are there uses in life to which such studies are indispensable? The arguments advanced in previous chapters for the associative use are familiar enough to be obvious. Nevertheless, the associative retrieval of contents in the imagic-conceptual store, despite the laws of association, is highly indeterminate. The content of the imagic-linguistic-experiential store depends on a host of variables that accompanied their deposit in the store. Frequently, we cannot recall the circumstances of that deposit. Can general education be justified by its associative potential? There is an air of imprudent investment in depositing so much in the bank of experience when the availability for its withdrawal is so unreliable. Can schools afford it?

The argument for such an investment for the interpretive returns is more plausible than for the highly unpredictable associative use, but is not obvious. Will study of the disciplines come to our aid long after we can no longer pass school examinations in them? Nevertheless, proponents of general education ask the schools to stake considerable time and financial resources on the expectation that it will.

Although skeptical about study that is not applicative, professional schools prescribe courses the direct application of which is only putative. That lawyers may need political science to interpret situations that can become legal problems is understandable, but that engineers and medical personnel had better study political science and sociology, let alone ethics, is only now being taken seriously by professional schools. Law, architecture, medicine, and accountancy find their graduates enmeshed in socio-philosophical issues that they can no longer dismiss as none of their business. Was the rejection of the separate but equal doctrine by the US Supreme Court in 1954 a legal, sociological, psychological, or ethical issue? Malpractice suits are remoralizing the professions.

The 1980 and 1984 elections in the United States may have been a reaction to the comingling of so many issues that their import for the life of the citizen was lost in a maze of technicalities. The Republican

Party pledged simplification of these complexities by allowing the market to free economic issues from what the editorial writers of the *Wall Street Journal* call "tedious moralism." However, the professions rightly suspect that they cannot turn the clock back too far. Social issues are mixed because social reality is mixed. Professionals will have to learn to mind other people's business in order to mind their own.

The first response to the new needs was to introduce new courses in the social sciences or the humanities as professional prerequisites. One would have thought that the college's undergraduate curriculum already included such courses. However, not all courses listed under sociology or philosophy will be "of use" to the engineer, lawyer, or physician. These future professionals are not expected to become sociology or philosophy scholars, i.e., to make applicative use of these disciplines.

That this is not an altogether new problem in professional education is witnessed by Cicero's discussions on the education of the orator.

> For when after the establishment of our world-wide empire a
> lengthened peace secured to us the enjoyment of leisure, there
> was hardly a young man of any ambition who did not think that
> he ought to put forth all his energy to make himself an orator.[1]

However, contrary to common opinion, Cicero argued that oratory and eloquence are not acquired by apprenticeship, but require study of many arts. Verbal fluency without a wide knowledge of many subjects he characterized as "worthless and even ridiculous." "My own private opinion is that no one can be a real orator in the full sense of the word unless he first acquires a knowledge of all the great subjects of human study."[2]

This knowledge, now as then, has to be more than a random associative resource; it comes closer to the interpretive use of schooling. The need is for contexts relevant to understanding the non-engineering aspects of engineering, the non-legal aspects of lawyering, etc. Each academic discipline can be regarded as a distinctive stencil that imposes its design on a problem. The stencils called biology, chemistry, mathematics placed on a piece of lung tissue yield different descriptions and suggest different explanations.

It would follow on this hypothesis that the lack of formal study of a discipline should manifest itself as lacunae in reading materials that presuppose images and stencils that presumably had been studied in school.

The search for research

Plausible as the theory undergirding the uses of knowledge may be, school people are understandably interested in empirical evidence for it.

In 1973 Keith M. Kershner and Bruce G. Baron of the Research for Better Schools, Inc., in Philadelphia, wrote a research proposal to the National Institute of Education seeking support to explore the developmental nature of the Interpretive Use of Schooling. The project envisioned (1) the development of a "theoretical and methodological framework for research in this field" and (2) a series of mini experiments. The conceptual framework was to be studied by a consortium of scholars in a number of academic fields. It was expected that the uses of knowledge schema could also facilitate research on Michael Polanyi's concepts of "personal" or "tacit" knowing and their implications for education. The results, they argued, would have significant implications for career education.

In communication with Kershner and Bacon, I suggested that the performance of individuals receiving no schooling or those in non-disciplinary or inter-disciplinary programs would vary from those enrolled in traditional courses. The project was not funded for reasons best known to the Institute.

In 1974, Michael F. Haines, of the State University of New York Maritime College, Bronx, New York, reported on a study of "The Uses of Knowledge as Determinants of College Curriculum" at the annual meeting of the American Educational Research Association in Chicago. A questionnaire was devised which included over 100 selected response items. Content validity of items representing the four uses of knowledge was established by the consensus of expert judges. The instrument was piloted to refine the wording of items and to sample the variety of responses. The population was established as all college and university teachers in New York state. For the sample, institutions were chosen at random from blocked categories of public and private two-year colleges, four-year colleges, and universities. Departments were chosen to represent the three major discipline types: humanities, social sciences, and natural sciences, and invitations to participate in the study were distributed through department chairmen. The data analysis is based on the responses of 234 faculty members representing 20 institutions and 58 departments throughout New York state. Data were coded for electronic processing which included tabulations, correlations, analyses of variance, and comparisons of means.

Respondents were asked to rate the importance of examples of knowledge use. Ratings were obtained for each example stated as a goal for students majoring in the respondent's discipline, for non-majors taking a service course or distribution requirement, and for students studying other disciplines as majors. In the respondent's own discipline, the scores for the replicative and applicative uses of knowledge (the specialist uses) were subtracted from the scores for the associative and interpretive (the generalist uses). This figure plus a constant yielded a number describing the extent to which a scholar can be called a generalist according to his beliefs about the uses of knowledge.

Respondents were asked to rate the importance of the several uses of knowledge. Those rating the generalist (associative and interpretive) uses more highly than the specialist (replicative and applicative) uses received a high generalist score. In rating the uses of knowledge as goals for their own disciplines, the derived score is designated Gl (for "generalist"). Gl was correlated to the respondents' agreement or disagreement with a series of statements about curriculum and instruction in colleges. The correlations were significant (S) or highly significant (HS)

According to the abstract,

> This study determines the preferences of college teachers for the associative, replicative, interpretive, and applicative uses of knowledge. Those preferences are seen as inputs to a curriculum development system and their relationship to outputs, curriculum and instruction decisions, are shown. Adherents of the generalist (associative and interpretive) uses over the specialist (replicative and applicative) uses state they rely less on traditional modes of instruction. Generalists more than specialists identify themselves as generalists, stress general goals, and support interdisciplinary courses and programs. The discipline of the teacher is a significant independent variable while institutional type is not.

These studies demonstrate an interest in testing the usefulness of distinctions implied by the uses of knowledge classification. To test more directly the validity of the hypothesis that "forgotten" materials learned adequately in school may still function in post-school life, the author with the help of a Spencer Foundation grant undertook a number of case studies.

Case studies

Case studies were designed in which eight graduate students with different undergraduate majors were asked to respond to five short selections from a metropolitan newspaper, plus a poem by Sylvia Plath. No attempt was made to correlate the responses with the biographies of the subjects or a host of other possibly relevant variables, although a good deal of biographical information was volunteered. The study was undertaken to test whether a more systematically controlled experiment was warranted. The newspaper selections included (1) a paragraph entitled "A Look at Venus on the Full Shell," concerning an argument between the National Organization for Women and the International Astronomical Union regarding the naming of some features of the planet after famous women in history, in addition to mythological ones, (2) an item on the current state of the economy that touched on the effects of tax policy, consumer price indices, inflation, etc., (3) a report on experiments to determine whether neutrinos have mass, (4) a report on *Dark Elegies*, a non-narrative dance by Antony Tudor, recently revived by the American Ballet Theater, and (5) an article on recent trends in archeology. The poem was Sylvia Plath's "Mushrooms."

The subjects were a (1) male law school student with a baccalaureate in history, (2) female law school student with an undergraduate degree in business, (3) male graduate student in educational research with a BS in Physics and a minor in astronomy, (4) female with an AB in English literature enrolled in a Master's program for creative writing, (5) male first-year student in MBA program who had taken a history of art course and an introductory philosophy course, (6) male with an AB in music education, now doing graduate work in the same field, (7) male with a baccalaureate in journalism and religion, doing graduate work in religious studies, (8) male undergraduate, double major in English and German literature, graduate work in German literature.[3]

The method required two stages. Stage 1 was a self-report in which the subject was provided with the printed texts and a set of questions, one at a time, and asked to sit alone in a room talking into a tape recorder about whatever came to mind. Stage 2 was an interview by Dr Shirley Johnson based on a schedule of prepared questions relating to items the subject talked about during Stage 1.

In Stage 2 the subject was asked to record name, age, present field of study, bachelor field of study, minor fields, courses in poetry, art, aesthetics, physical sciences, life sciences, specific texts used, as well as materials read for relaxation, items that had special influence, etc.

In the follow-up interview, the subject was questioned about allusions to other learnings, emotional sets, types of thinking. What does this passage, line, mean to you? How might you use this information? What came to mind as you read this?

The data, so to speak, are the complete recordings of all the subjects including a remark by a former business school graduate to the effect that "Sentences like 'The economy is struggling with a 30 billion dollar deficit' make me laugh ... I don't know anyone who knows what 30 billion dollars means. I certainly don't."

To the same phrase, another subject responded: "I've got to learn about income taxes and money. Here I am a woman struggling to be independent and this is my one main area of illiteracy, and I'll never make it unless. . . ."

These responses were made to questions on a particular sentence in the selection on the economy. The remarks made during Stage 1 strayed over even wider territory. Yet such variability and degrees of relevance are the very point of the study. To reproduce them in their entirety would be too much of an intrusion in this volume.

The following samples will illustrate the methodology of the study.

J. A male graduate student in German literature with an undergraduate degree in English and German literature.

"Venus on the Full Shell"

Self report
At first is puzzled by point of the article, but infers that the issue had to do with naming features of Venus after women. Can't make out what "they hope to gain by this," and notes that ERA "won't gain anything. . . . It's just, perhaps, politically a step for NOW."

Is reminded of his thesis research on Hauptmann, who wrote in the period (1890–1910) when the women's movement was "very big." Thinks Hauptmann's treatment more naturalistic and realistic than what NOW is trying to do.

Recalls mythological connotations of Venus and thinks that inasmuch as she was the goddess of childbirth that NOW would want features of all planets to get rid of sexist names and name them after both men and women.

Title, he thinks, refers to "Boccacio's Venus on the Half Shell" (hard to tell from tape whether he meant Botticelli) but notes that NOW might be making fun of the "seductive" appearance of Venus.

Comments on non-sexist syntax, e.g., gentleperson, etc. . . . selection makes him think of a science fiction work, *Venus on the Half Shell*, by Kurt Vonnegut, a satirical look at futuristic society, especially at women. Would like to find out who wrote the article and relationship of author to NOW — whether male or female.

Follow-up
Studied mythology in old English literature and also in Latin course in high school, but remembers something in junior high school about mythology and read a good deal about it. Had a project in it; took material from encyclopedias.

Learned about NOW when vice-president of the student govern-ment and talked to two girls who organized women's movement. Interested in it, especially in western part of North Carolina which had racial problems in mid-1970s and so equality and inequality tend to get overemphasized: refers to "token blacks" in every office; thinks if ERA is passed, tokenism and "selective" hiring to meet requirements of the law would take place.

Allusion to title came from course in art history ... remembers the painting, but thought the painting he had in mind was a mock representation of the original in the book by Kurt Vonnegut (under the name of Kilgore Trout) and instead of being at the seashore, Venus is out in space.

The economy

Self report and follow-up
Strongly negative reaction to the article on all grounds. Two themes are stressed: the incompetence of economists and the incompetence of government with regard to inflation and tax policies. Reads about economics in the papers but, as he says, "I don't enjoy this type of material."

Neutrinos

Self report
The remarks indicate more familiarity with the technical terms than in the article on the economy. Some of this he attributes to experience on a nuclear submarine while serving in the navy; some reflects formal school instruction, but the associations veer from technical points to social consequences and issues in nuclear power and weapons. Notions such as mass, particles, grand unification scheme, Einsteinian equations are mentioned as if there were a general awareness of the theories and experiments involved but no technical and systematic knowledge.

Follow-up
The formal schooling in this area came from three months in a school in California and three months at a prototype plant in Idaho; the first three months were pure theory, dealing with what went on in a reactor. Notes that there is no direct observation of neutrinos and other sub-atomic particles, but is vague about the sort of evidence used to substantiate their existence and effects ... he suspects that there is a lot of guessing. Cites the use of "may" as indicative of this uncertainty. This sensitivity to the difference between the indicative

and subjunctive moods he attributes to his studies of both English and German language.

Dark Elegies

Self report
This article on the ballet by Tudor elicits a lot of comment, most of it positive and almost excited. Among the themes touched on are: the importance of innovation; ballet as a means of communication; the period in which the ballet was composed and performed; characteristics of art in various periods; modes of expressing character and emotion in literary and dramatic forms; revivals; references to German writers and dramatists.

Follow-up
Amplifies on the topics mentioned in the self report; although he is not familiar with the ballet, never having seen one on the stage, except the *Nutcracker* on television; is very much interested in it as a mode of artistic expression and most of the references are related explicitly to German literature. He is especially aware of the break with tradition in the early part of the twentieth century and cites Brecht.

Returning to the theme of communication, he refers to his own difficulties in communication and his efforts to correct it. Cites courses in writing, and experience with writing papers; leads to remarks about how professors get published and the requirements for being published.

Archeology

Self report
Has read about archeology and would be interested in reading about it. Is bothered by the reference of the article to human beings as wild animals as were other hominids. Doesn't quite understand how dispersion from African woodlands and savannahs occurred and comments on the lack of continuity and transition in the writing of the article. The selection reminds him of visiting museums in Germany and archeological remains there, and this reminds him of cave paintings in France, and how archelogical finds build up to improve knowledge about history of man. Does not quite understand significance of the statement that there has "been a shift in the objectives, because the cream has been skimmed off."

Follow-up
In the self report he had made a distinction between the history of

man and learning about that history. Seems not to have remembered this, but in trying to explain it turns to the difference between the "process of archeology" and the "goal of archeology" and notes that the selection shifts from the latter to the former. Returns to his tendency to examine writing in terms of grammatical and logical structure and cites experience in school and his efforts to improve his own writing. Keeps returning to stylistics. Has read only one book on archeology, but does not remember the name; thinks it is *Masada*, and tells some of the findings. Had a chance to go on a dig but passed it up; too expensive.

Questions on the "cream being skimmed off" elicit recollections of travels in Italy and visit to Pompeii and many random observations; also references to lots of reading when young *All About Series.* Stories of finds and mysteries interest him.

"Mushrooms"

Self report
Makes a long set of remarks on the poem touching on the following themes: the negative mood of the poem — Sylvia Plath "pessimistic, suffering, inferiority." Style of composition — uses of metaphor, *apparent* spontaneity in choice of words. Later he interprets this to mean a simultaneous appearance of spontaneity that conceals a high degree of structure.

Interprets Sylvia Plath's psychology in terms of her father and his being a German; the Second World War.

Follow-up
The follow-up session dwelt a good deal on how J. learned to approach poems as he does. He cites courses in poetry, also the *Bell Jar* and things he had heard about Sylvia Plath, her suicide, cruel to her father. In poetry courses he learned to analyze a poem, into stanzas, lines, syllables, etc., as well as for theme, to try to experience the mood of the poem.... Gets emotionally involved when reading for enjoyment, and tells how he has tried to do some writing of a fictional sort himself, and the problem of evoking emotion.

K. First year law student; female; bachelor's degree in business. No courses in poetry, art, art history, aesthetics, physical science or biology. Reads for relaxation (before starting law school) *Time, US World Report* and books on best seller list that her roommate got. Book that influenced her was *Atlas Shrugged* (cannot remember author).

"Venus on the Full Shell"

Self report
Article strikes K. as "idiotic" and "trivial." Finds "gentleperson's agreement" irksome and feels the same way about other manifestation of de-sexist syntax. Seems unable to comprehend why the issue is discussed and what it is really about; "I don't know a single planet feature, anyway."

Follow-up
Has not read much NOW literature and says she knows nothing about the organization. Confirms that she has had no science courses, for some reason, not even in high school. Apparently in skipping a grade she missed out on the general science course. Reads a little about science; has no taste for biological topics, but "things like stars interest me."

She had noted in the self-report that the sentence "The announcement coincided with the unveiling by the National Aeronautics and Space Administration" didn't seem to go with the rest of the passage and re-affirmed this on the follow-up attributing this to her experience with a religious publication. This made her sensitive to consistency in style and matters of basic English rules and structure. Follow-up session closes with interviewer asking about the title and explaining the academic joke when it was clear that K. had no notion of what it meant.

The economy

Self report
Does not seem to understand such terms as consumer's index, windfall profits tax, oil conservation fee, and inflation rates. "Social security" makes her think of "retirement." The reference to the 1976 inflation rate of 4.8 per cent being "tranquil" reminds her of daffodils (probably jonquils). She is not quite sure for whom such articles are written.

Follow-up
Interviewer tries to clarify responses to "consumer's index." K. says she did learn about it in her business courses, but in terms of what an average family would spend.

As to the statement that "large-scale tax increases are not the appropriate solution for a badly slumping economy," K. said that she thought this was true. There ensued an interchange on the role of money in the economy and the effect of taxes. K. cites several theories about the role of money and taxes, but has no opinion about their usefulness or validity. Says she did not find the article useful because, "There's too many things thrown in there that isn't explained ... so many figures and no explanations ... I don't like articles like this, I usually read them though." She thought that she felt pretty much the same way about government publications.

Neutrinos

Self report
Would glance over this article even though "I have no background in science — don't understand the article, don't understand what neutrinos are, even how you pronounce it...." Don't know what grand unification is — vaguely familiar, maybe from high school, wonder who's paying for all this; what makes them think of it; pictures of men in white with glasses. No really good discoveries for years; fascinated by really original ideas. "Seemingly weightless particles' like volcanic ash or dust in the air, don't know what they are ... that fill the universe." Where does the universe start? Astounding. How can it be? Wish I knew what "grand unification" means; guess effect on physics would be revolutionary. Why isn't gravity in a "single theoretical framework"; wish I knew that.

Follow-up
The follow-up revealed little not in the self report. The general image aroused was "dust." The unification idea did not arouse thoughts of Einstein or relativity, and her illustration of ideas that were "good" discoveries was Edison's work on the light bulb, or the airplane. Impressed by math, people "sat there and figured out about triangles, and areas inside them, and all that kind of stuff."

Dark Elegies

Self report
Struggled through this article; would never read this on my own; doesn't make me think of much, except image of people jumping around on stage; never seen a ballet; never seen an opera, and confident never will.

On Mr Tudor's gift for making specific characters reveal their emotions on the stage, K. is at a loss as to how "you reveal emotions, if you just go through the steps of a dance, especially since aren't these supposed to be planned out?" To the statement, "All these works are plotless" K. says "I don't know what's going on when I see them on TV ... think I saw the *Nutcracker* once ... didn't have much effect, I guess. Why is evocation underlined?"

Follow-up
Merely reaffirms all the comments made in self report.

Archeology

Self report
The topic of archeology makes K. think of a friend who is an archeologist; she doesn't want to put in the time that it took her friend to become one ... "super-herd instinct...." People don't like to think of themselves as herds; when I see herds I think of cattle.... "Several million years ago." The idea of that is fantastic; writer seems to be projecting image of primitive man out there against all the animals; also telling us that "we're wild animals."
    Didn't know towns began 6000 years ago.
    Doesn't like the word "looting" in connection with archeological digging; "doesn't seem like looting to dig things up."
    Reference to "glamor sites" evinces comment that digging things up is not glamor.

Follow-up
Confirms remarks in self report, but adds that she has two friends in archeology — one digging in Arizona; another runs a museum in California, and this gives her some understanding of what is involved, although she didn't know one had "to go through all this" to run a museum. She thought she understood the article and would read it for background general information. Repeats that very long periods of times (several thousand years ago) strike her as "fantastic."

"Mushrooms"

Self report
"Foot in the door." ... Didn't know mushrooms were that violent, and reminded of evergreens in front of her house and the mushrooms that grew up through the pine needles.
    "Shoulder through holes." She doesn't like the "We" sticking out in the middle there and comments that the whole poem brings out a lot of images and "if we leave title 'Mushrooms' off of it and let someone read it could they tell what you're talking about? Are they talking about mushrooms?"

"Crumbs of shadow" — "interesting, but it doesn't mean anything."

"We are shelves, we are tables, we are meek, we are edible."[4]

"'Shelves' — That's what I think when I see a mushroom ... a shelf and a table; is reminded of a place called Santa's Village with mushrooms all around that you sit on. Overall 'thing's kind of creepy.'"

Follow-up

Tape not always audible, but confirms self report items. She doesn't like poetry, has never read poems by Sylvia Plath; did not have poetry in high school; sensed that much of the language of the poem was figurative and that "most poems take something ordinary and ruin it."

Analysis of responses

The results of the eight case studies, I believe, confirm the thesis that without formal study in a field the response to a general article on a topic in that field is likely to be randomly associative. Associations from language, reading of newspapers and magazines, and personal experience suggest themselves as relevant to the passage. These, in turn, arouse attitudes toward the subject and recall episodes that may have formed such attitudes. For example, most, if not all, of the subjects had some familiarity with NOW, the planet Venus, and the space probes, but it was information gleaned from routine mention in the press, television news, and the like. The reference of the headline, "A Look at Venus on the Full Shell," in only two instances prompted recollection of the Botticelli painting, and in these instances the encounter took place in a college course on art appreciation. The astronomical issues were rarely discussed scientifically except by those who had studied astronomy. Many of the comments on NOW referred not to the astronomical aspects of the issue but wondered why NOW could find no more important issues on which to take a stand.

Schooling, it would seem, had contributed generously and variously to the allusionary base, but more to the associative use of that store than the interpretive. The appropriate conceptual structures necessary for the translation that interpretation entails had not been studied formally and therefore left no conceptual residue, no stencils by which the phenomena could be structured or translated. Only those who had studied astronomy and physics could interpret the scientific references in the selection.

A group of faculty members from a number of disciplines read the protocols and met to discuss them. After a volley of disparaging remarks about the responses, they ruminated for quite a while on what academic studies should contribute to a proper response. There was no agreement as to how the subjects were construing the materials and the psychological and logical theories that would explain it. They suggested that a study employing much more structured methodology that would isolate the relevant variables would be worth doing. However, there was little doubt that eight young people who did not have the benefit of college education would have responded to the selections differently. The difference in response to the poem by the one subject who was studying creative writing and that of the other subjects clearly indicated the difference in the effects of general and professional study.

Alan C. Purves, Professor of English at the University of Illinois, who wrote an extensive analysis of the responses to the poem, said in conclusion:

> As one reviews these eight responses, one gets a sense that each reader in his or her own way "learned" to read poetry in a particular way, whether it be to take it literally, to see it as a springboard for association, to see it as a basis for interpretation. Each of the modes of approach has its basis in some aspect of schooling, and each of the readers has retained what was taught as well as a few pieces of information that can be brought to bear. The information, however, appears to be less firmly implanted than the way of reading a poem and the way of thinking about it — as nonsense or as a serious art form.
>
> You accept the notion of schemata in reading, one can see that each of these readers has acquired a poetry reading schemata that is put into use when a new poem is confronted. It is difficult to determine whether this "use of learning" should be considered application or interpretation. It is a mode of thought applied to interpretation of new texts. Clearly, however, it appears to be powerfully apprehended and summoned into use almost without being willed.[5]

CHAPTER 4

Tacit knowing or knowing with

The argument for uses of schooling other than the replicative and applicative ones rests on such evidence as the case studies and observations described in the previous chapter. Theoretically, it poses a challenge to the positivist thesis that all knowing is restricted to propositions that can be verified by observation. Thus "John learned algebra in high school" is true if, and only if, John can solve typical algebraic problems by the methods practised in school. Success on the test would be convincing evidence that John could (a) replicate his learnings and (b) apply them to problems that had not been practised but were of the same type as those on the test. Whether the test permits the inference that John would also be able to use algebraic formulae for solving problems of mensuration in life situations is not so certain, because application of principles requires familiarity with a class of existential situations that only the professional is expected to achieve.

The epistemological argument for the plausibility of associative and interpretive uses of schooling rests on the possibility of knowing *with*, as distinguished from knowing *that*, knowing *how*, and in some instances knowing *why*. The theory that seems most consonant with the notion of knowing *with* is that of tacit or subsidiary knowing developed by Michael Polanyi.[1]

Although I was not familiar with Polanyi's work on tacit knowledge when our book on the secondary curriculum was written,[2] it was clear from his discussion of the subject several years later[3] that it was the type of knowing which supported the distinctions among the four uses of schooling.

Later, I found the notion of tacit knowing helpful in explicating the difference between truth (warranted assertion) and credibility (warranted belief).[4] The essay argued that truth as scientifically determined can no longer supply even the well-educated citizen with a rational basis for decision on the major social/political problems of the day. Debaters on nuclear energy, nuclear war, environmental issues, economic and foreign policy, affirmative action, among others, seem to have little difficulty adducing evidence for equally defensible, albeit incompatible judgments. Parties to disputes denounce simplistic solutions and leave the citizen with a strong suspicion that there are no other kinds. In such a predicament problem-solving techniques have to be supplemented by a touch of fideism, the sources of which are more likely to be tacit than explicit. The grounds for warranted belief and commitment are likely to be found in willingness to risk much — perhaps everything — on the existence of objective values or ideals, grounds for which science cannot supply. What could be more objective evidence for commitment to a cause than the corpse of a martyr to that cause? Yet all it proves is the existence of a belief in values, not of the values themselves.

In a somewhat similar vein Hans-Georg Gadamer distinguishes scientific thinking from hermeneutical understanding. The former, he believes, is knowledge of general rules that can apply to particular situations. Rationality in action is knowledge about means to an end that is not in question. In interpretation goals are not given in advance. The meaning of a text is produced by the interpretation of the reader, and the reader is changed by that interpretation. The rationality of interpretation, according to Gadamer, is embodied in Aristotle's view of practical wisdom, which is preferable to the efforts of Socrates and Plato to reduce it to technical or theoretical reason, efforts based on intimations rather than proof of the existence of an ultimate reality.[5]

Furthermore, if, with Descartes, one presses the disparity of the bodily and mental series of events and the consequent separation of thoughts from things, the problem of knowledge turns into a puzzle philosophers can neither solve nor leave alone. This does not mean that the dichotomy between mind and body, thoughts and things, is not deplored. Ryle's work[6] is typical of modern attempts to banish the ghost from the machine, as were John Dewey's assaults on the dichotomy. This and other objections to the separation are well taken, as the logic of discourse and the deliverance of intuition plainly attest, but appeals to logic do not really banish the ghost from the machine. Intimations of reality, to use Polanyi's term, make us revert almost insensibly to thinking of persons as ghost-like machines or machine-like ghosts.

Some products of mind, whether in science, philosophy, art, or religion, make connections with reality that are below the surface of everyday behavior and consciousness. Intermittently, they disturb that surface. These intimations of the real, the important, the ultimately valuable that Polanyi refused to banish from what he called "personal" knowledge elude the positivistic barricade.

Judgments of credibility, for example, depend more on character traits such as candor, honesty, loyalty to ideals, than on the logical evidence for what is asserted. Dissonance between explicit claims to virtue and hidden motives is taken as a lack of credibility. By restricting their responsibility to observance of special rules or laws, not only the business world but the lawyer, physician, politician, and even the educator can evade moral and social responsibility. Limiting one's responsibility in this way is a species of amoralization or demoralization.

Such demoralization is endemic in a modern technological culture, because technical standards tend to take the place of moral ones. If a procedure or venture is likely to be profitable, the intrusion of moral considerations beyond non-evadable law is regarded as moralistic irrelevance. This trend is facilitated by the translation of all values into monetary equivalents, i.e., price. Thus, if a painting, a tennis match, a palimony suit, and a cannon are all priced at $250,000, they are equal in value, and the need to invoke other types of value judgment is unnecessary.

Among the many reasons for the lessening of public fervor for social and political reform in the 1980s was the lack of credibility of some of the reformers. For example, the battle for racial equality, when led by well-to-do white lawyers and tenured professors, seems less credible than street demonstrations by the minorities themselves. The reformers would gain credibility with the public if they gave up their own jobs or their salaries to unemployed minority members. Corporation and university presidents solemnly announcing the need for salary cuts and other sacrifices by their employees would improve their credibility if the announcements were not made to the press in luxurious executive suites. Complicated arguments invoking the wisdom and justice of Adam Smith's Invisible Hand may be sound theoretically, but they do not sound convincing. Token sacrifices do not pass for genuine ones. A 10 per cent cut in wages may inflict real misery on the hourly wage earner, but not on the corporate executive who has ordered the cut for the good of the firm, the industry, and the nation's economic health, not to mention the ultimate prosperity of the worker himself.

The persistent mistrust of pious sentiments expressed by persons in high places is grounded, not on economic theories or facts, but on a tacit sense of fairness rooted far more deeply in the human psyche than any economic or political theory. Individuals being rewarded in proportion to their contribution to society is fair, but there is doubt that the competition is always fair. The image of competitors in a race all lined up at a well-defined starting mark satisfies the sense of fairness, even when it is known that some competitors may do much better than others. But if in the second race the winners of the first are given head starts, the sense of fairness is impaired, and with it the credibility of the advocates of free and untrammeled competition.

One may wonder where and how this sense of fairness originated. There seem to be few signs of it in the lower animals. There the

Darwinian principle of natural selection goes on its way without organized opposition. Nor does it stem from theological theories about God's justice, for that is as inscrutable as His other mysteries. If a conjecture is in order, one might consider the innate aesthetic sensitivity to the principle of balance. Not only is balance critical for the body and the interactions of many bodily processes, but we perceive the world about us as also exhibiting such balance and coming to grief when the balance is disturbed. Balance is essential to fairness. When it is disturbed in buildings, they shudder; when disturbed in human relations, society feels tremors that may become quakes. This sense of fairness together with the numerous objects and activities that exemplify it may be regarded as a subsidiary factor that integrates and structures the focal situation.[7]

Clues to credibility, e.g., the willingness of the person to live by what he/she professes, tend to be tacit rather than explicit. The blood of the martyrs is more impressive as proof of sincerity than of the merit of their cause.

Much of what is called moral education operates by way of maxims learned explicitly in youth, which become part of the tacit imagic-emotional-noetic store *with* which the rightness of action is judged in mature life. Intimations of the fecundity of an idea, a theory, or an ideal for unrealized possibilities, which Polanyi attributed to personal knowledge, may also be grounded in the noetic-imagic store, once taught explicitly but becoming tacit in post-school life.

Attribution of arcane knowledge to the learned professions and the belief that they will intercede for all who need their knowledge in crisis situations regardless of station and financial circumstance also depends on a tacit mystique. Similar tacit factors convince citizens that their political party is dedicated to a transcendent cause and should be supported despite arguments and evidence to the contrary.

Polanyi's distinction between focal and tacit knowing also helps explain the difficulties in moral education. In trying to determine the "right thing to do," we marshall moral principles and try to apply them to choice of action. Or we identify the situation as one to which an accepted code of conduct applies. Social classes are often characterized by such codes. This cogitation can be performed explicitly, often habitually, sometimes logically. However, sooner or later, the question of why we believe moral principles or trust codes of conduct will be raised. What will determine the answer? For some, a rehearsal of the philosophical arguments learned in ethics courses may yield a viable and satisfactory answer, but satisfactory logical proofs may not be emotionally convincing. One believes the proof, but finds it uncomfortable to live with. The reasons for this discomfort may not be stated or even statable in explicit terms, perhaps because of attitudes produced by conditioning in earlier times and reinforced by subsequent social pressures. These conditionings now function tacitly to affect the judgment demanded by the explicit conditions of judgment. To paraphrase Kant, without conditioned attitudes towards right and wrong, moral education is empty; without the principles of ethics, it is blind.[8]

On knowing with

A body of scientific propositions contains what Gilbert Ryle calls "knowings that" and "knowings how." These cognitive skills include not only reading, writing, and computation, but also problem solving, critical thinking, judging, etc. By the use of these skills, the subjective contaminants of sense perception attitudes can be neutralized, and objective truth attained. Among these contaminants, the previous experience of the learner is the most familiar and among the most important, especially in the domain of value education. The differences induced by the influence of home, social class, and other institutions are so great that value education in a public school seems to be theoretically and practically a hazardous and perhaps fruitless enterprise.

However, the *laws* of association are not wholly idiosyncratic or randomized and while some associations are adventitious, some like the skills, images, and concepts studied in school may function in a more orderly and predictable manner. Furthermore, there are those who argue for the need to posit a logical and cultural *a priori*, e.g., those of Kant, Durkheim, Marx, and some of Bacon's idols, which presumably is uniform for the race or for certain samples of it. The capitalist ideology, according to Marx, distorts the judgment of all (save Marxists) who live in a capitalistic system. According to Kant, we have no choice but to experience the world under the forms of space, time, and the categories of the understanding.

For education, the distinction between diverse individual experiential contributions and those that claim to be uniform for the race is important. The existence of idiosyncratic influences should not be regarded as a sufficient reason for renouncing instruction in those structures of thought that are not idiosyncratic, viz., the structures of the intellectual disciplines. Among these disciplines are those that deal systematically with the intellectual, moral, aesthetic, and religious values. Once these disciplines begin functioning tacitly they make value education more than products of cultural conditioning.

It is tempting to argue that the educational concerns with instruction are psychological rather than epistemological. To the extent that education is concerned with providing the optimum conditions for instruction and learning this is true, but what if the psychological theory intersects with epistemological theory? For example, Jean Piaget's theory of learning was "rediscovered" in the 1960s primarily because his notions about the structure of logical thought were consonant with the post-Sputnik concern with science, mathematics, and logic. However, Piaget was interested in the development of logical structures as stages of child development so his work is referred to as "genetic epistemology." Indeed, one is tempted to say that Piaget provided psychological support for some of the Kantian categories, e.g., he notes that the idea of the conservation of substance (as distinct from notions of weight and shape) could not have come from perception.[9]

Educational epistemology can be thought of as a logical assessment of the schemata needed by the learner to comprehend scientific, historical, and literary materials; of the way such materials are used to interpret problems such as the degradation of the environment, poverty, etc. However, as earlier chapters have tried to show, these materials are not necessarily used as originally learned. For example, in the early 1940s a test was designed to measure the American public's knowledge of American history. It resembled tests that might have been given at the end of a secondary school course in the subject. The public failed the test so badly that a hue and cry was raised to teach more American history or to teach it better. The American Historical Association (by way of one of its officers) was incensed by the observation of this writer that only *idiot savants* would remember the sort of facts asked for unless their vocation forced overlearning them, and that the results did not prove that the American public would necessarily be ahistorical in its interpretation of situations to which history was relevant, despite the test results.

For example, suppose the situation to be understood was the participation of the United States in the First World War. Courses in American history would have taught names, dates, causes, and results of a number of wars, both those in which the United States was an active combatant and some in which the nation was involved indirectly. The courses would undoubtedly have discussed relations between the United States and other nations. Granted the details of such instruction were virtually forgotten over the years, the more general understanding of the causes of war, their conduct, and results will not necessarily have been extinguished. However, given test items that call for replicative recall only, the poor performance by the public is understandable and perhaps forgivable.

One would not expect a physician who had never studied biology or chemistry to read medical journals that presupposed some knowledge of these disciplines; yet it is equally difficult to believe that such a physician would do very well on end-of-course examinations in school courses 10 years after having passed them in college days.

The most straightforward attempt to found a curriculum on the replicative use of schooling was illustrated by the Committee on the Economy of Time in Education set up by the National Education Association in 1911. It recommended that nothing be taught in school which could not be traced to its use by the general population in their daily tasks. In the 1920s educational research sought out the words most commonly used in private correspondence, the errors in spelling most frequently committed, and type of arithmetic problems encountered in this or that occupation in a particular region of the country. Only these qualified for inclusion in the curriculum.

All of this made sense if the primary use of schooling were replicative or applicative. It makes much less sense if the major use of schooling, especially of general education and the foundational studies in in the professions, is interpretive and associative.

Nevertheless, the received doctrine is that the replicative use is the typical, virtually paradigmatic use of schooling; that what is replicated is a learned connection between a stimulus and a particular response. That this is the received doctrine is evidenced by the ubiquity of the slogan "down with non-objective objectives." This requirement was defended on the grounds of objectivity; that only what is publicly testable can claim objective status and be the subject of rational discourse among both theorists and practitioners. Thus Ayer says:

> We know that if . . . a mystic had really acquired any information he would be able to express it. The fact that he cannot specify what he "knows," or even devise an empirical test to validate his knowledge, shows that his experience was not a genuinely cognitive one.[10]

The uncritical acceptance of the positivistic theory of knowledge and education leads to the paradox of praising general studies as essential for all members of the school population, while admitting that most of what has been studied and successfully tested in school will have disappeared from memory in post-school life. The notion of tacit knowing dissolves the paradox.

1 Tacit knowing is distinguished by Polanyi from focal knowing. When two slightly different pictures of the same object are viewed in a stereopticon, the final image is known focally, i.e., seen in the center of the visual field. According to Polanyi, while seeing the unified picture, there is a tacit or subsidiary awareness of the two separate pictures of which the unified image is the resultant.

2 It is to be noted that we cannot simultaneously have both focal and tacit awarenes of the same object. Further, in the act of comprehending an entity by means of its components, the parts achieve a vectorial quality, i.e., the bearing of the parts *on* the entity comes into focus and thus are cues to the meaning of the entity.
3 The laws governing the structure of the parts are not sufficient to describe the principle of their integration. One is reminded of the theory of emergents that acquire properties not contained or displayed by their constituents.
4 The act of knowing involves an effort at integration by the knower.[11]

Polanyi lists a number of types of tacit knowing: skill attainment when a number of discrete motions are integrated into a joint performance; reading of a physiognomy in which the several features are clues to the expression of the face; the problem of classifying specimens by unifying a number of characteristics. Sense perception itself requires the integration of a number of sense impressions, without being aware of the brain processes that produce them.

How valid is this theory? Gestalt psychology with its emphasis on figure-ground, closure, whole-part organization of experience seems to involve tacit knowing. That we cannot reduce sense perception to simple sensation also seems to bolster the theory. However, the more familiar argument comes from his explanation of scientific inquiry. Polanyi argues, for example, that Copernicus had no reason for preferring his system to that of Ptolemy, and many reasons for not doing so. He, Kepler, and Galileo made their discoveries, Polanyi argues, because they believed in a certain vision of reality and not the other way around.[12]

If the hypothesis of tacit knowing has probability, it gives strong theoretical support for the associative and interpretive uses of schooling as a way of avoiding the anomalies and paradoxes that follow from the assumptions that the primary uses of schooling are replicative and applicative.

To restate the Polanyi position, one can say that a pupil (P) uses school learnings (L) as subsidiary cues to interpret the more comprehensive situation (S). If Polanyi is right, during this act of interpretation, we are not aware of (L) focally, for we are using (L) subsidiarily. If Polanyi is correct in this central thesis, then the school inputs need not be found in the outputs in their original form.[13]

What, then, do we know and think with? The intellectual disciplines embody schemata that bear on a wide domain of experience. The humanities and arts do likewise. Not only do they constitute resources relevant to a vast array of life situations, they also project a vision of reality and a continuity of commitment to that vision. We think *with* this culture and we think *with* it even to revolt against it. The consensus of the learned at any given time probably is the best operating criterion for the school curriculum. The educated mind thinks *with* the conceptual and associative resources of this consensus, and the school needs a criterion of truth no less fallible than that which the learned themselves employ.

Another ingredient in the prescription for "thinking with" is the desire for coherence, for a vision of reality that supplies an integrative power to thought, feeling, and action. What is the school to do about this ingredient?

The teaching of science has not brought it about, albeit technology is making a strong bid for that honor. Specialist scholars' desire for coherence stops at the boundary of their speciality, and specialist scholars in the humanities are not always exceptions. Students who persist in looking for something called "wisdom" in their classes may be referred to the counseling clinic. An overarching faith in a reality that will not frustrate the desire for coherence can be injected into school learning by the enthusiasm of the teacher, provided the enthusiasm does not take the place of intellectual competence.

However, there are other ways. One is the careful study of the *discoveries* in science and art, which, if Polanyi is right, will reveal the urge to coherence. Another is to incorporate into school learning the great molar problems that necessitate interdisciplinary thinking. Just how disciplinary learnings can be used to do this is still a mystery, which, one may doubt, will be cleared up by holding more interdisciplinary conferences. Yet if the drive to coherence directed the development of the disciplines in the first place, it would be odd if this vision could not be built and sustained by the study of these disciplines. Nevertheless, the possibility of some other organization of learning providing the urge to coherence cannot be dismissed.

We can summarize schematically the uses of schooling as follows:

For a person (P) to understand a situation (S) is to order it to a larger or more general context, not merely to recollect learned items. Interpretively, (P) uses former learning to classify (S) as a member of some species or to hypothesize that (S) is the cause of an event or to recognize that (S) falls under some principle or law. In short, (P) upon encountering (S) interprets it by constructing some context into which it should belong. This context can be a logical, causal, axiological, or aesthetic network. We then say that (S) has become more intelligible to (P). Suppose that (S) encounters the statement: "In times of economic depression, spending in the public sector has to be accelerated." (P) might interpret it by providing a context drawn from Keynesian economic theory. How many of the details of that theory would (P) have to recall to do this?

Suppose (P) is asked to appreciate (S) when (S) is a poem or a picture of the sufferings of persons in ghettos or prison camps. Some replication of learned experience will occur, but primarily (P) is called on to instate a mode of perception accompanied by imaginative reconstruction. Because virtually all aesthetic expression is indirect and metaphorical, (P) has to call on previous experience for images and meanings plausibly associated with (S). In aesthetic interpretation one uses learnings replicatively and associatively as subordinate clues within a larger perceptual-imaginative framework. These associations are not random, but neither can one predict from the framework just which items will be reinstated. If this were possible, art would be a form of science, or at least a form of direct communication. That all school learnings to count as learning must be used replicatively makes a shambles of all attempts at aesthetic education.[14]

CHAPTER 5

The role of imagery in uses of schooling

As we drive along the turnpike, we come upon a signpost reading "Boston 150 miles." If our destination is Boston, the sign gives useful information, and even if we are not planning to stop in Boston, it augments our knowledge to be informed that it is 150 miles ahead. This is a simple example of symbols conveying information, provided the reader is familiar with the English language. If the sign read "260 kilometers," some American drivers might have to do some calculating to get an idea how far away Boston really was. The sign is printed in what Susanne Langer called "discursive" discourse. The words denote entities that belong to a species to which a name has been assigned. Or they denote mental procedures and rules by which the symbols are to be combined to yield appropriate connotations.

Such language usage is characteristic of Ryle's "knowing that," a kind of "knowing how" to perform the procedures signalled by the language, a kind of knowing that can be verified by empirical tests. That the message *really* says "Boston 150 miles" can be verified by other qualified readers. That Boston is *really* that far away usually can be verified by the odometer. Construing these phrases is an instance of the associative use of knowledge in response to learned cues. Previous experience has created an allusionary store awaiting retrieval by the proper clues.

When a statement requires not only understanding of the words and their syntax but of concepts as well, then simple association is not sufficient. Thus "A straight line is the shortest distance between two points" requires not only a translation of the words, but an understanding of the geometric generalization being asserted, as well. A whole system of concepts has to be brought into consciousness — the definition of a line, point, etc. — and their spatial relationships. Interpretation involves the associative uses of learnings, but primarily the reinstatement of learnings about relations among concepts. As has been indicated, interpretation is a kind of translation — the positioning of a situation in a conceptual framework. These conceptual schema, roughly speaking, are the domains of the several academic disciplines, each employing distinctive entities and relations, paradigms of use, etc.

The sign reading "Boston 150 miles" requires interpretation. It entails understanding the concept of distance and its measurement. Miles are not kilometers, and while experienced travelers can form rough ideas of about how far 150 miles would be, e.g., the same distance as between two familiar cities, anything more precise would require thinking and reckoning that is more than or somewhat different from recollecting this or that fact or circumstance. Interpreting the sign requires something different from random associations retrieved from the store of memory.

Another mode of associative use is instigated by aesthetic perception. Suppose on arriving in Boston and seeking a restaurant, the travelers come upon a sign in script lettering of gold on a clear white background reading "Cafe Royal." The sign announces that food is served there, but it also conveys the cluster of ideas "an expensive place to eat." Here cognitive perception is supplemented by a visual image, what Langer called a "presentational symbol," or "expressive form," an image that conveys information by its appearance. To be sure, words are printed on the sign and give the clue to the nature and function of the establishment — being a restaurant. The word "Royal," if taken literally, would be misleading, except under very special circumstances. The *appearance* of the lettering and the background, however, arouse associations that yield the judgment, "This eating place is expensive."

In the same fashion, the dark cloud not only suggests the possibility of stormy weather, but "looks" threatening; an angry face also can look threatening, somewhat like a thundercloud. The raising of the flag at Iwo Jima not only conveyed information about American soldiers raising a flag over a battlefield, but by sheer appearance conveyed a complex of emotions; it looked patriotic, strong, and victorious. The French national anthem, the *Marseillaise, sounds* a call to arms; *God Bless America* does not. Experience is replete with images perceived by the senses that convey human import by their very appearance.

Such images are often presented by mountains, rivers, flowers — natural objects — by buildings, dress, and deportment, but preeminently by works of art, i.e., appearances contrived to convey human import, not by referring to objects other than themselves, but by their very appearance. Mt Everest, for example, can be identified on a map, has certain geological features and history. But by its very appearance Mt Everest can be characterized as grand, lofty, challenging, dangerous. These are not physical qualities but human ones.

A pain in the neck, the eye, the arm may not be the image of anything; simply a localized sensation of pain and nothing more. It may be characterized as strong, dull, sharp, but to qualify as an aesthetic image, the pain has to be *like* or *of* something. To say "Tom is a pain in the neck" is to invite the hearer to form an image of Tom acting *as if* he were staging an attack on the nerve endings of a person's neck. Odors are usually classified as fragrant, putrid, sweet, etc. The fragrance of the morning is a figure of speech because mornings are not odors, albeit the air one breathes in the morning might be scented. To create images out of sense qualia, one must resort to metaphor, a figure of speech.

Aesthetic perception, therefore, is a special sort of cognition. It might be called a knowledgeful feeling which is also feelingful knowledge. It is the perception by means of the senses of an image that conveys human import. Feeling, after all, is our most primitive register of import to the organism. The "lonesome pine" conveys lonesomeness by means of the image of a tree, a pine tree. The aesthetic experience, accordingly, combines what analytically are distinct and disparate. Knowledge connotes the capture of the nature of objects in propositions. Feelings, on the contrary, are scientifically understood as nerve impulses traveling along pathways inside the skin and not normally open to direct inspection. The ability of an image to externalize a feeling so as to make it available for contemplation is the peculiar power of art to create and for the mind to perceive. The appearance is the message.

Aesthetic properties

The mystique of art has been the source of wonder and awe. It has created a sharp boundary between knowledge and art, knowledge and feeling, between art and everyday experience. In schooling it has meant a division between the arts and the academic subjects that has prevented the arts from achieving a permanent place in the roster of studies required for general education. To be sure, scholars write learned books on the history of art, the meaning of art, and role of art in society. This knowledge, however, has been thought too arcane for the school curriculum, while the making of art — drawing, painting, singing — was a skill that many could try, but only an accomplished few would pursue once their critical faculties were developed. Repeated reforms demanding that art become a required subject in the schools flounder as imitations of studio training or simplified versions of art appreciation are suggested as models of art programs.

What art education needs is a method of perceiving and analyzing aesthetic properties that can be taught to children in the elementary grades by the classroom teacher. After all, elementary teachers are not specialists in geography, science, mathematics, or any of the other subjects they are required to teach. Until this becomes possible, the arts will remain nice but not necessary. There is a sense, therefore, that to take arts education seriously entails instating it as the fourth R. A method of doing so was developed in an aesthetic education seminar held in Los Angeles during the summer of 1975 under the auspices of the Office of the Los Angeles County Superintendent of Schools and the National Endowment for the Humanities and under the direction of Dr Frances D. Hine. In that seminar there was an opportunity to experiment with a mode of analysis based on my 1972 Kappa Delta Pi lecture that had been published under the title *Enlightened Cherishing* by the University of Illinois Press.[1] The method is based on the supposition that subjects with normal sense organs can perceive aesthetic properties, and that children even in elementary grades can be taught to do so systematically.

1 Sensory properties

Colors, shapes, lines, pitches, volume are themselves analyzable. Color can be perceived as hue, value (extent to which a color is dark or light; black is the absence of color and white is the presence of all colors). Another dimension of color is intensity (bright, medium, and dull), transparency in various degrees (translucent, opaque).

Shape can be described as organic, inorganic, open or closed, geometric, etc. Line can be analyzed in terms of length, width, direction. Texture (a surface quality) is rough, smooth, wet, dry, hard-soft, coarse, etc.

2 Formal properties

The ways in which the sensory properties are organized are sometimes referred to as design. Among the more familiar categories are theme and variation, repetition, balance, different types of rhythm, dominance, and crowning them all — unity in variety.

3 Technical properties

Although knowledge of the means and methods by which the aesthetic object is created is not essential to the proper perception of the object, there is considerable interest in such matters, even by non-specialists in art production.

4 Expressive properties

These are the most important properties of the aesthetic object, to which the other properties are means. They are also the most difficult to describe. Nevertheless, we can observe and characterize the human import portrayed by the aesthetic object by noting the type of language in which they are describable. Thus *mood* language uses such descriptive terms as glad, melancholy, joyous, whimsical, playful, haunting, austere, cheerful, dreamy, etc. Or the object can be described in terms of dynamic states — such as conflict, relaxation, suspense, strong, weak, high or low energy. Finally, the expressive properties can be characterized by idea and ideal language. Nobility, courage, heroism, freedom, majesty are among a long list of ideas and ideals.[2]

This approach challenges the common contention that a work of art cannot be analyzed systematically, and that unless a magic transfer of meaning and significance to the viewer automatically and immediately takes place, proper appreciation is impossible. Especially does it challenge the contention that only artists and educated critics can construe works of art.

It has been called aesthetic scanning designed to serve as an introduction to aesthetic perception. Its pedagogical advantage lies in that the reports of what is perceived can be verified by other perceivers. Any assertion or attribution of a property to the object is open to the demand that the property in question be pointed out, i.e., located and identified for others to perceive. Given reasonably healthy sense organs, it is not unreasonable for A to assert that *American Gothic* has sensory properties x, y, and z, and, if necessary, point them out for B's perception. The same claim can be made for the formal and expressive properties, albeit in this department mere pointing does not necessarily settle the claim. If A asserts that *American Gothic* is "solemn," there may be no single identifiable property to which one can point by which to convince the doubtful observer. A can only name the mood or idea he or she perceives and invite B to do likewise.

5 Phenomenological objectivity

The view that the aesthetic object and the aesthetic experience are subjective through and through is a serious challenge to the notion of aesthetic cognition, i.e., feelingful knowledge and knowledgeful feeling. It belies the fact that aesthetic phenomena do enlarge and often alter how and what one thinks and feels about a piece of music, a landscape, a painting, or sculpture. This means that aesthetic experience does have some causal efficacy, which, in turn, seems to imply some sort of being or existence, some ontological status. To by-pass the vexing problem of the ontological status of mental states, it may be suggested that the meanings portrayed by the aesthetic image have phenomenological objectivity, whatever its ontological status may be.

The principle stipulates that whatever is perceived in the aesthetic objects must exist (phenomenally) *in* the object and is not merely projected on to the object by the observer. That it does so exist is demonstrated by the ability to point to some perceptible feature of the object. Partners in such a colloquy may disagree on the nature and import of what is observed, but they should be able to agree on what properties are being discussed. If I attribute the enigmatic expression on the Mona Lisa's face to the conformation of the lips and eyes, it should be possible to point to these conformations and have them observed by others. Phenomenological objectivity does not prove ontological objectivity, but it does furnish a method for exploring the aesthetic properties of the object with some semblance of objectivity.

Pedagogically, this distinction and the perceptual analysis based upon it is a valuable tool in aesthetic education. Aesthetic scanning can be carried on with children as young as five years of age, and has been used in a number of projects in arts education, including the Getty Institute for Educators on the Visual Arts, directed by W. Dwaine Greer. It directs the attention of the learner to the object where the sensory, formal, and expressive properties are to be perceived. Scanning prevents the use of the object as a cue to a premature report on how it makes the observer feel. It inhibits the tendency to use the aesthetic object as a stimulus to free association, reminiscence, and, last but not least, the intentional fallacy, the musings about what the artist had in mind or intended to express.

The systematic scanning of the aesthetic object to analyze its sensory, formal, and expressive properties builds the alphabet, so to speak, of aesthetic "literacy." It is only the beginning of aesthetic education, but a necessary one, and one usually passed over. The fleeting glance at a picture is enough to set off a stream of comments that reflect a great many things, but not necessarily or even usually the properties of the object itself.

For the truth of the matter is that in viewing a painting or listening to music we rarely perceive much of what the artist or composer created. Most of our perception in ordinary life is selective rather than complete. We use the appearance of the object as a cue or signal. Aesthetic perception is distinctive in that what is in the image cannot be overlooked or ignored. If it can be ignored, then it has no place in the work of art. It is a flaw in aesthetic unity. For most individuals aesthetic perception of works of art has to be cultivated deliberately.

The allusionary base

The role of imagery in learning is both direct and indirect. Directly, it is the immediate perception of patterns of sounds, shapes, colors, and motions that convey meaning. Indirectly, the meanings conveyed by images affect the significance of language, concepts, values, and ideals. They constitute a distinctive component of the allusionary base, the resource of the associative and interpretive uses of schooling.

By the allusionary base is meant the complex of images, concepts, memories of all sorts available to provide meaning to words and events. It would be reasonable to find references to the Declaration of Independence, the Bible, George Washington, Abraham Lincoln in the allusionary base of a US citizen. Among educated readers one would expect familiarity with some characters and episodes of Greek and Roman mythology as well as some acquaintance with the major concepts of the physical, biological, and social sciences.

In so far as the allusionary base lacks these components, hearing or reading material to which they are relevant is reduced to word recognition. Encounters with a foreign language illustrate the difficulties caused by gaps in the allusionary base. With the help of a good dictionary one can decipher every word in a phrase and yet not comprehend it. Poetic and colloquial language are especially dependent on the allusionary base for appropriate images. Poetry, for example, requires extensive footnotes to supply imagery for allusions to remote times and places, as well as to unfamiliar characters.

The allusionary base may well be the matrix of reading comprehension. Decoding the text does not insure understanding. Dictionaries, while of great help in defining words, present reading problems themselves. Difficulties of comprehension, of course, are occasioned by the circumstance that the written word as such does not provide its own connotation. Nevertheless, words are not always arbitrary symbols. This becomes evident when the etymology of the words being defined is noted in the dictionary. The word "transport" to one who has studied Latin may evoke images of "carrying across" whether it is used in a sentence such as "The wheat was transported by barge down the Mississippi river" or in a description of how in her dreams the heroine of a novel was "transported" to ecstasy. In as much as many, perhaps most, words have origins no longer familiar to the modern reader or speaker, these images of their original meanings are no longer part of the allusionary base.

Alasdair MacIntyre makes a similar point in discussing the translatability of different languages into equivalent meanings. He notes that such translation provides phrase books for travelers rather than the adequate semantics for natural languages. "Concepts are first acquired and understood in terms of poetic images."[3]

Are there "natural" meanings in sensory states? According to Fred Dretske, there are.

> If a sea snail doesn't get information about the turbulence in the water, if there isn't some state *in* the snail that functions as a natural sign of turbulent water, it risks being dashed to pieces when it swims to the surface to obtain the micro-organisms on which it feeds.... Of what possible significance is it to be able to handle symbols for food, danger, and sexual mates, if the occurrence of these symbols is wholly unrelated to the actual presence of food, danger, and sexual mates?[4]

The natural meanings as internally sensed to which MacIntyre and Dretske refer are even more directly asserted in Isaiah Berlin's discussion of Giambattista Vico's claim to direct knowledge of our internal states.

> When we say that our blood is boiling, this may for us be a conventional metaphor for anger, but for the primitive man anger literally resembled the sensation of blood boiling within him; when we speak of the teeth of ploughs or the mouths of rivers, or the lips of vases, these are dead metaphors or, at best, deliberate artifice to produce a certain effect upon the listener or reader ... men sang before they spoke, spoke in verse before they spoke prose, as is made plain by the study of the kinds of signs and symbols that they used, and the types of use they made of them.[5]

Perhaps the most famous dictum on the relation of concepts to sensory experience is Kant's "Concepts without percepts are empty; percepts without concepts are blind." But is sensory experience by itself really blind? Not if the preceding discussion has plausibility. More plausible is the dictum that concepts without percepts are empty. Can we have imageless thought? If we can, then it does not need the aid of imagery. Mathematicians sometimes claim that mathematics can dispense with imagery, but what is meant by the "beauty of a theory" or the "elegance" of a proof without a sensory (aesthetic) image? Diagrams are used freely in expounding mathematical problems and every equation by its equal sign invites the reader to instate the formal properties of balance — an aesthetic principle.

The allusionary base provides resources for the connotation of words that go beyond denotation, their function as names. The ability of the pupil to point to a dictionary in response to hearing the word "dictionary" is sufficient for denotative purposes, although in the reference room of libraries it may not be — there are too many big books that look like dictionaries. Denotational definition helps identify the object, but it may not yield a meaning for the phrase: "He is a walking dictionary."

Some images are of objects found in the world — houses, flowers, clouds, people. These can be perceived as merely denotative much as a photograph or a diagram might be. In the arts, however, images are expected to be connotative, images not only of recognizable objects, but of their human import as well.

Language and the allusionary base

The most striking difference that one study found between the language usage of educated and non-educated groups was that the "vulgar" English group seemed linguistically poverty stricken. A word such as "get" is employed 10 times as frequently in the Vulgar English letters as in those of the users of Standard English. "The user of Vulgar English seems less sensitive in his impressions, less keen in his realizations, and more incomplete in his representations."[6]

Linguistic poverty may be both a cause and consequence of meager associative resources. Reading of literature in general and poetry in particular is directly affected by such poverty. The cognitive uses of language are also influenced by the volume of what Herbart called the "apperceptive mass." Science as well as art depends on the imaginative activity of the mind. Although language may not be able to label all that the imagination conjures up, it is still our best catalogue of human experience. Lack of linguistic resources may be a token of poverty of thought and feeling as well.

Much of our experience is influenced by the concepts and images encountered in the study of literature. As one traveler put it, "Had my first view of the Lake District in England or the Forum in Rome not conformed to the images of these places formed by my school studies, I probably would have rejected the realities rather than the images." The images in which the poet, novelist, artist, composer, as well as the historian, perceive the times in which they live are among the most potent resources for the educated response to life problems.

For example, one of the major social problems of our time and for the time to come is that of old age. Psychologists, sociologists, biologists, and economists are wondering about "what to do with mother." Old age has been a standard topic for essays, together with friendship, honor, virtue, etc., and who is to say that William Butler Yeats in *Sailing to Byzantium* has not contributed to the understanding of old age when he said:

> An aged man is but a paltry thing
> A tattered coat upon a stick, unless

> Soul clap hands and sing, and louder sing
> For every tatter in mortal dress[7]

Although imagery is a prime factor in the associative uses of schooling, and although art is among the most important sources of such imagery, it is not the only one. Suppose one comes across the term "Elizabethan Drama." This term is place holder for such associations as: Queen Elizabeth, Mary Queen of Scots, Henry VIII, Shakespeare, knights, battles, and Tower of London. Henry VIII is a veritable freight train of associations: historic, erotic, religious, and political.

Poetry, understandably, relies heavily on imagery for its effects. There is a type of prose, however, that also depends on figurative use of language. Slang, the poetry of adolescents, and oratory, the poetry of politicians, also utilize the imagic uses of language. That Senator So-and-So is a "wimp" may be immediately perceived in a number of images: the fall of the voice toward the end of a sentence, a limp posture, hesitant gestures, are visual, kinaesthetic, and auditory images of weakness.

The dependence of oratory on aesthetic images has been emphasized from the time of Demosthenes. Among the requirements for the teaching of rhetoric in the times of Quintilian and Cicero was the composing of imaginary speeches that might have been given by certain historical or mythological figures. Retelling of fables vividly was also among the prescribed exercises. Apparently, one of the keys to efficient oratory was a store of images, concepts, and affective patterns that would lend their power to the oration.[8]

That reliance on aesthetic images by orators is not confined to the classical past is witnessed by President Reagan's State of the Union message delivered February 5, 1986. In it the President used more than fifty figures of speech to convey how he felt the nation ought to feel about the past, present, and future of the nation. Among them were the following: "Go forward, America, reach for the stars," "A land of broken dreams," "A lumbering giant," "A mighty river of good works," "Freedom is on the march," "But we cannot stop at foothills when Everest beckons," and "I'll take the heat."

Obviously, the perception of the images conjured up by the figures of speech not only gave meaning to the language but contributed an emotional aura that made them effective means of communication. This impact depended on the listener's associative store of images of meaning and the ability to ignore departures from literal usage. To construe: "Freedom is on the march," for example, requires considerable conceptual and imaginative resources. Freedom is an abstract quality denoting both a physical and moral state. A prisoner is physically unfree, but may still be morally free, if he can exercise the will to choose. It is not clear which type of freedom was intended, but there was little doubt that the phrase would elicit the appropriate image of the feeling the President was trying to arouse.

The effect of metaphors and other figures of speech depends on a willing suspension of literal meaning in favor of images arising from associative resources. With effort and ingenuity one might trace the ingression of these words and images into a person's allusionary base. A quicker way is to ask a non-English speaker to come up with the needed image by translating "Freedom is on the march" into his/her native tongue. A Frenchman, we might suppose, might start humming "*Marchons, marchons,...*" and envision a call of the citizenry to battle. Whether a Turk would respond with similar imagery is not so clear; he might construe freedom in a way that the speaker did not have in mind.

"I'll take the heat," a bit of slang, is an image of different sort. To a foreigner, it might be puzzling, even if each word were given the correct lexical definition. Why would the President promise to accept heat? What has heat to do with the situation? Young children might also be puzzled by this use of language as they might be on hearing someone say, "If you can't take the heat, stay out of the kitchen." How would one explain "The buck stops here" to a young child or a foreigner?

Explanations take time and attention to understand. A figure of speech, by contrast, works, if it does work, instantaneously, if the listener has the requisite imagic-linguistic resources. A key ingredient of schooling is reading materials that invoke imagery and test it.

The perennial concern with illiteracy is occasioned by reports such as that of one University of Texas study in 1975 which estimated that one in five adults could not read well enough to understand a medicine bottle warning, a job notice, or a school report card. This is shocking, for it means that 20 per cent of the adult population may be unable to respond to very important linguistic messages that affect their daily lives. That illiteracy has been called by some experts America's hidden problem is disturbing because of its practical consequence, but it is puzzling as well. It is puzzling because the teaching of reading is one of the incontrovertible priorities of the schools, one that is reinforced by the exigencies of living as well as official requirements. Probably no aspect of schooling has received more attention from researchers, publishers, and teacher training institutions. By now, one might suppose the technical problems to have been solved. It may be that attention to imaginative poverty in early childhood will yield important insights into "America's hidden problem."

This extended discussion of the allusionary base or the associative and interpretive resources it contains is intended to make the role of imagery in diverse aspects of experience clear and explicit, even though it does not work explicitly. It is no accident that we sometimes speak of picturesque language, but much of the daily use of language is far from picturesque and therefore dull and often poorly communicative. To have the ability to use language aesthetically, i.e., to convey import by its ability to frame evocative imagery, is an important factor in personality; perhaps important enough to consider as a vector in personality and personality adjustment.

Imagery and judgment

The associative use of imagery in comprehension of language, extensive as it is, does not exhaust its role in everyday experience. This needs to be addressed directly because terms such as imagery, aesthetic experience, etc., are so often identified with art. This masks its role in the discourse of judgment, the discourse of everyday life. The ingredients of the allusionary base weave images and concepts together in a stream of premises and inferences that are not ordinarily studied in logic courses. Yet they constitute the bulk of everyday judgments.

From early childhood we are schooled to beware of appearances. We are warned not to believe promises of advertisers that their products will have the merits portrayed in their appearance. Nevertheless, the array of decisions we make on the strength of appearance is vast and varied.

To begin with, our judgment of persons tends to be based on appearances. We cannot hope to investigate the facts behind the appearances to test their accuracy as premises for valid conclusions. We are told, for example, that in the world of business each worker is expected to conform to an image appropriate to his/her role. Clothing, style of speech, posture, gesture portray the model performer in the role. We have neither the time nor opportunity to investigate the "truth" of the image. In most of our social and vocational encounters the appearance is the premiss for the judgment. "Tom has a weak chin ... not good executive material" may prevent finding out if in fact Tom could or could not make a good executive.

As we pass a long row of houses in an unfamiliar neighborhood, we tend unconsciously to make the appearance of buildings, lawns, motor cars in the driveways premisses for judgment about the financial level of the residents, their status in society, and, not infrequently, their character. A house fronted by a lawn that is scraggly, luxuriant in weeds and scattered stones is judged to house civic slobs or perhaps a clutch of college students exploiting the benefits of community housing. The same house and the same lawn carefully mowed, with the weeds growing in neat circles and the stones in rows, give rise to a quite different judgment about the inhabitants. Yet the only discernible difference is the arrangement of the weeds and stones, a difference in formal properties. A standardized image serves as a premiss for conclusions not only of the character and social status of the inhabitants, but also of the price that the property would bring on the market. The appearance of a bank building must convey an image of solidity and trustworthiness; a negative image will require strong evidence of fact to counteract it.

A further example of the potency of the aesthetic image for interpretation is the change in the frontage appearance of residences. Not so long ago private residences were built with an entrance facing the street. The entrance made concessions to the need for ornamentation of the front door, a porch, and a pathway to the door. The kind and amount of such ornamentation depended, of course, on the size and grandeur of the building, both of which were designed to portray the economic and social status of the inhabitants. The carriage house and later the garage were in the rear of the main residence with a separate driveway.

In more recent times, however, the front of the residence is likely to feature the entrance to the garage. Not infrequently, the garage, usually a double one, is nearer to the street than the residence itself. The entrance to the house is likely to be curved to the side of the house. Some residences have no path to the front door at all, but utilize the garage driveway for that purpose. The garage has become as much a status indicator as the residence. A highly-priced motor vehicle in the driveway conveys an unambiguous message.

Conversely, a street lined with parked motor vehicles indicates a neighborhood of lower economic status, because it announces that there is insufficient garage space for all the vehicles, and in some instances no garage space at all. Economic status is symbolized by the amount of space available for the car as well as the price of the car itself. It would be thought strange, for example, to leave a Mercedes or Jaguar regularly parked overnight on the street, just as it would have been thought strange in former days to leave one's coach and four tethered to a hitching post on the street night after night.

Passers by on residential streets may be innocent of the literature on the dynamics and characteristics of social change, but they make quite accurate judgments by appearance as to what counts in social and economic status. The motor car has assumed a role in our culture similar to that of houses, of servants, forms of entertainment, etc., as indices of status. Space itself has always been one of these signs, and today space for the car is an important factor in one's residence and place of employment. Parking for the car is a major problem in large cities as well as an item of considerable expense. The amount of space that in the United States has to be preserved for the motor car, not only in the form of garages and parking spaces, but also for interstate highways, would in all probability match the territory of a small country.

Clues to social attitudes are found in the disappearance of the front porch where once one exhibited oneself to the passers by and expected others to do likewise. Today this tacit invitation to exchange greetings and the doings of the day has been withdrawn. Leisure time is spent inside the house or in the rear of it on a patio designed primarily for privacy. Where building codes permit, walls are often built around the residence signalling the desire for privacy and perhaps a warning to those who might be tempted to violate it. One thinks of the resemblance to the moat around one's castle.

How much of this change signifies fear of intrusion from thieves, drug addicts, and mindless hooligans and how much a desire for privacy is hard to gauge, probably a mixture of both. The point, however, is made clear by the visual images created by the building landscape; it needs no formal verbal explanation to be understood.

The importance of standardized images in social intercourse is accentuated by the loss of image standardization. There was a time when tramps, ne'er-do-wells, and decent citizens could be sorted out by their appearance — clothing, grooming, posture. In a strange city or on a lonely beach a stranger's appearance would yield a dependable clue as to whether or not he was to be treated with suspicion. The lack of standardization of appearances makes one ponder whether the ill-dressed stranger approaching us should be treated as a potential mugger or a remnant of the hippie generation. Even the police, who are supposed to be sophisticated in such matters, can make serious mistakes.

The celebration of freedom from stereotyping is easily accepted in principle, but without its assistance every particular situation has to be judged not by appearances but by investigation of facts. This converts numerous routine situations into matters of careful inquiry — no longer routine. The wish to live in an environment where appearances are reliable indices of character, status, and circumstances is strong indeed; stronger as a rule than the ideological commitment to diversity. Conversely, when appearances send messages that are not true, social maladjustment is around the corner. The deception may be innocent, but it can have serious consequences nevertheless. The de-standardization of images as clues to individual and social characteristics makes for interesting variety, but it also increases the cognitive strain on social adjustment.

Manners are considered to be standardized behaviors for standardized situations. This, to be sure, reduces the strain of interpreting social situations. Social intercourse, however, may impose an aesthetic obligation as well. If in daily life many persons whom we do not know and who do not know us are subjected to our appearance — visual, tonal, kinaesthetic — are they not entitled to expect us to present what D. W. Gotshalk characterized as "an appearance interesting to perceive?" Appearances "interesting to perceive," however, are aesthetic images that convey human import. Hence, there may be a sort of aesthetic duty that goes beyond manners, viz., to present behavior patterns interesting to contemplate and conversation that is interesting by virtue of its form as well as its substance. Conversation can be an art without becoming artificial.

In each of the value domains — the economic, health, recreational, associational, civic, intellectual, religious, moral — aesthetic images are used to portray attitudes and behaviors that typify ideas and ideals within that domain. We speak of Mr X being "the picture of health." Presumably there is an appearance typical of the healthy. We recognize the life styles of various socio-economic classes by standardized images of their houses, dress, and demeanor. In the civic sphere the eager reformer, the conservative protecting the status *quo ante*, the wily politician, the white knight serving and protecting the people are familiar stereotypes who convey by their appearance the values they represent.

In each domain the allusionary base is raided for images and concepts with which to construe the phenomena of that domain. Stereotypes and departures from them make their impact on our thinking and feeling *via* these images and whatever systematic knowledge we acquire by education. Social, political, economic, health, religious, intellectual values all have their aesthetic and cognitive dimensions. Conservatives and revolutionaries utilize concepts and images to preserve and strengthen their convictions and programs and to undermine competing ones.

What studies will provide the learning materials needed (1) to construe the appearances of events in a given domain and (2) to master the conceptual frameworks by which the several domains are structured for understanding?

Schooling in the arts

What is the relevance of imagery in learning to programs of schooling? If, as has been argued, the aesthetic image, which has been defined or characterized as a portrait of feeling, is not only the central feature of art, but also an active factor in the use of language, in all forms of perception and cognition, in judgments from the simplest to the most complex, then it would be strange indeed if it did not impinge on education.

The associative and interpretive uses of schooling have been described as building up and drawing on the resources of the allusionary base, the source of subsidiary or tacit knowing. If images have a central role in this process, why have the arts not attained full membership in the required curriculum of the schools and colleges in this country? Recent legislation mandating such studies only underlines their peripheral status, but does not answer the question as to why such legislation was necessary.

The explanation lies in the status of the arts in our culture and perhaps in the cultures of most western countries. To put it bluntly, the fine or serious arts[9] have traditionally been the concern of the upper social classes. They were the patrons of art and their children were given lessons in whatever art forms their culture prescribed. A young lady destined to be introduced to society might attend a young ladies' seminary. There she would study French, receive lessons in piano and voice, learn embroidery and painting water colors. These accomplishments were requisites for entrance to and membership in that society. Children with talent would be given private lessons and subsequently enrolled in a special school where advanced study would be available. In short, the upper classes did not depend on public schools for tuition, just as artists did not depend on the ordinary citizen for patronage. In earlier times, arts in the schools were more likely to be urged by American industries that depended on good design in textiles, jewelry, clothing, etc. The idea that the children of all social classes needed to have schooling in the arts, therefore, is revolutionary, even in as democratic a society as that of the United States.[10]

Another obstacle to making art a part of the prescribed curriculum was the method of instruction, fashioned after the model of studio training. Highly suitable for prospective artists, it requires talent and unusual determination to master the skills of performance. This disqualifies it as a general requirement for a school population in which such talent is not evenly distributed. To be sure, talent for other subjects is not evenly distributed either, but whereas even a modest aptitude for reading or mathematics is useful and necessary, a modest endowment in producing art is neither necessary nor always useful. Accordingly, the arts and the instruction in them have not been regarded as either practical or necessary for the total school population, albeit highly desirable as electives in the secondary school and as quasi-recreational activities in the elementary grades.

The claims that art instruction provides the pupil with an opportunity to be creative and a means for self-expression are plausible and the outcomes laudable, but they do not lend themselves to the requirements of a curriculum of a school system, viz., systematic instruction in a field that has recognizable skill and knowledge components. Some schematism such as has been indicated for the analysis of aesthetic properties is required to qualify schooling in the arts as a regularly required subject feasible in the elementary grades. In the secondary years, a required curriculum would have to draw on the resources of art scholarship in history and criticism for content.[11]

If proponents of the arts were to argue that the school is a necessary avenue to the enjoymnent of art, it could be rejoined that never was art so accessible. Television, especially public service television, regularly provides a high level of music, dance, theater, and the visual arts. Radio also offers a generous fare in the arts. Furthermore, there is no lack of popular art and customers for it.

Fairy stories for the very young, popular music and dance for adolescents, and recollection of the art of their own adolescence for adults do not require regular formal instruction. To live in a culture is to absorb these arts; not to do so is a symptom of social maladjustment. Furthermore, the arts, being praised and celebrated as sources of enjoyment, could hardly qualify as necessities, however desirable they might be for those who had access to them. The strategy of turning the arts into a required school subject, therefore, has to rebut the explicit argument and the implicit belief that, although the arts are precious and wonderful, they are not necessary. This rebuttal takes the following form:

1 The aesthetic experience, of which enjoyment of art is a species, is unique and therefore requires special instruction. This wards off the proposal that the arts be taught as illustrative of subjects already in the required curriculum, e.g., using a famous painting to illustrate events discussed in history or social science. This ploy requires an aesthetic theory of some kind. There is no lack of them, as any good anthology's table of contents makes evident. Nor is there any lack of debate as to their adequacy. Aesthetics as a formal field of study is highly developed but although usually available in departments of philosophy is not generally studied by most college students, and perhaps not by all students in the fine arts department. To take the arts seriously as candidates for general education requirements would require as much theoretical sophistication about formal aesthetics as there is about the theoretical underpinnings of the other subjects of instruction. This requirement would apply not only to the arts specialist but to the classroom teacher and the members of the school board as well. It must be granted by all concerned that

the aesthetic experience has unique characteristics and a unique function.

2 To counter this argument for uniqueness it can be objected that a field so special as the aesthetic experience lacks relationship to all the other value domains — a curricular oddity, so to speak. The proponents of the arts must, therefore, be ready to show the relationship of imagery to a wide range of human life and learning, as this and other chapters in this volume have tried to do.

3 The school authorities, having been persuaded that the aesthetic experience is unique and yet relevant to all values, may ask why formal tuition in art is necessary. Could not generous exposure to offerings of the already existing agencies for art production and display educate the public? Could not the schools discharge their obligation to aesthetic education by offering their premises and student bodies as audiences for art performances? To counter this offer, one has to argue that the arts have structures analogous to that of disciplines in the required curriculum, viz., a symbol system that has to be mastered, modes of perception that have to be cultivated, insight into concepts, and skills that have to be acquired. The aesthetic experience, in other words, is more than a spectator sport. It has skill and knowledge components that require formal tuition.

4 Granted that such skills and knowledge are required, could the standard brand of classroom teacher provide the instruction? Or would the school system have to hire a small army of artists and arts educators? Would not the cost of such personnel on such a scale render the whole program unrealistic?

To which it can be replied that it does not follow that the classroom teacher cannot teach the arts, if an appropriate methodology were developed for doing so. Accordingly, the controversy, real or simulated, comes to rest on the possibility of aesthetic education as a subject of instruction in which classroom teachers can be trained to the same degree of proficiency as they are trained in the other subjects of the curriculum in which classroom teachers are rarely specialists.

The crux of the issue, therefore, is the possibility of devising a methodology that allows the teacher to induct the learner at a fairly early age into the skills of aesthetic perception analogous to the analysis of the symbol system in reading, writing, and arithmetic, the fourth 'R.'

Aesthetic scanning makes this possible by systematically exploring and identifying the sensory, formal, and expressive properties in the aesthetic object. Figure 6.2, page 84 describes the method in some detail. A number of projects, among them the Getty Institute for Educators in the Visual Arts, the HEART project in Decatur, Illinois, and a similar one in Champaign, Illinois, have shown conclusively that classroom teachers can be taught to use the method with elementary school children. The key hypothesis of the method is simply that whatever is perceptible to the senses in an aesthetic object can be perceived and to some degree named and identified. The skills of aesthetic perception can be taught to the entire school population.

The method, simple as it seems, nevertheless rests on an even simpler hypothesis, viz., that if the artist put the sensory item in the work, the viewer is obligated to perceive it — otherwise it is otiose. If the object is a natural one, e.g., a sunset or mountain, there still is an obligation to note the properties that constitute it as an image portraying feeling. Once the skills of scanning are mastered, the curriculum can move to the historical and philosophical literatures in the field, viz., history of art and formal aesthetics.

This view of teacher preparation for art instruction in the classroom of the elementary school is not generally accepted by those college arts departments that provide the courses required for teacher certification in many states. On the contrary, it is perceived as a threat to the arts specialist who traditionally has given the instruction, or a sample of it, in the classroom and expected the regular teacher to supplement it with appropriate exercises. That many elementary teachers do not feel qualified to do this and are embarrassed by this feeling of inadequacy accounts for a good deal of the unevenness of arts instruction in the public schools. However, there is no reason why the skills of aesthetic perception (as distinguished from the skills of performance) cannot be made part of the pedagogical repertoire of every elementary school teacher.[12]

Until teacher training institutions provide the classroom teacher with the skills of aesthetic perception and its analysis, it remains for the arts specialist to undertake their in-service education. This would have the laudable effect of providing steady employment for such specialists, instead of being the first to fall victim to a budgetary crunch. This function added to the elective courses in art performance should provide full and steady employment to the arts specialist.

What has been noted as the role of imagery in the learning of skills and attitudes could be extended by analysis to the learning of concepts and values. Between the particular and the class intervenes an act of the imagination that gives rise to the notion and image of an aggregate of objects stripped of their individual characteristics. In other words, abstraction, the key operation in concept formation and conceptual thinking, depends on the ability to form an image of class characteristics. To be sure, once such an image is formed, it can be replaced with symbols of the class characteristics and reasoning can proceed by their use. The need for models and diagrams is witness to the role of imagery in the teaching of the most abstract and abstruse of the sciences and other academic disciplines.

The case is even more marked in the attempt to teach values. Values are norms or involve norms, and norms have also to be imagined, i.e., furnished by images of thought and behaviour. Ideals require similar acts of imagination and imaging. All of which argues for more explicit attention to the role of imagery in all phases of instruction, rather than confining it to rare experiences of creativity.

CHAPTER 6

The curriculum and the uses of schooling

If the notion of the four uses of schooling is plausible, it ought to have suggestions and perhaps implications for the construction of a curriculum for general education. Figure 6.1 provides a design for such a curriculum for grades 7-12. The secondary school may be the end of general education for many young people as well as a preliminary to its development in higher education.

The major parameters of such a curriculum — demands of the culture, uses of knowledge, and research in curriculum and learning — have already been discussed in varying contexts, and although the third is somewhat outside the scope of this volume, it is an important vector in the argument for this organization of the curriculum against others. However, the notion that bears directly on the uses of schooling is that of building cognitive and evaluative maps out of symbolic skills, basic concepts, developmental studies, value exemplars, and molar social problems.

These maps define the goal of general education as distinguished from vocational training. To a large extent, curricula in law, medicine, and engineering rely on general education requirements in the arts and sciences to provide such cognitive and evaluative maps. But they may specify special course requirements that, although taught in the liberal arts departments, may not be designated as general education requirements. Engineering, for example, may prescribe special course work in mathematics and law schools may want their students to have studied certain types of history. Such special requirements are expected to provide cognitive maps that will help organize problems of professional practice.

Evaluative maps are central in the claims of general or liberal education, but like the cognitive ones are directed to the needs of the individual as a citizen and for self-cultivation rather than for professional uses. However, every profession professes ideals (values) that justify its special duties and status. These values and norms have their theoretical roots in philosophy, ethics, and philosophy of religion. There is a sense, therefore, in which general education provides resources from which principles of professional ethics can be abstracted, an enterprise that in recent times has become entangled with the complex of legal principles invoked in malpractice

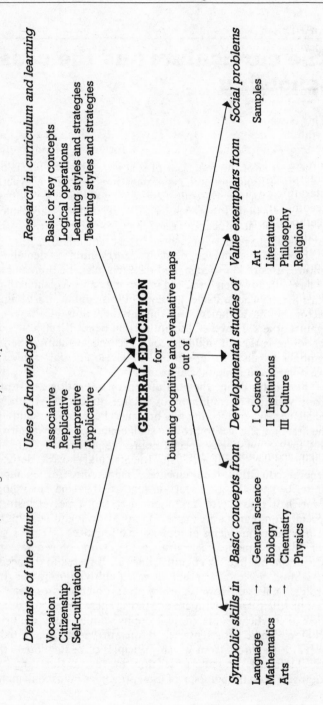

Figure 6.1 Design for common curriculum in general education (grades 7–12)
Source: H. S. Broudy, B. O. Smith, and Joe R. Burnett, *Democracy and Excellence in American Secondary Education*, Chicago Rand McNally, 1964, p. 160

suits. Courses in medical ethics, for example, are becoming a speciality in departments of philosophy and medical schools.

Symbolics of information

The entrance to an academic discipline is through a system of symbols. The three Rs are the most familiar of all scholastic symbols systems, and the necessity of mastering them for replicative use is altogether too familiar. The teaching of reading has become a large enterprise, with its own research apparatus and specialists. The literature on the teaching of reading is voluminous and how to teach reading at all levels and in all circumstances is the core of the methods work in the preparation of elementary school teachers. Coding and decoding the linguistic symbol system is the decisive criterion of success in the work of the public school. Complaints of employers that high school graduates cannot read, write, spell, and reckon are sparks that ignite perennial attacks on the public schools.

There is reason to hope that the advances in electronic technology, in one way or another, will help to meet this complaint. If coding and decoding a set of arbitrary symbols for replicative use is so important, then all the resources of technology ought to be invoked and massed to guide the drill and evaluation that replicative use entails. Technology plus inventive use of motivational psychology, which also might be programmed into the computer, one hopes will solve the reading, spelling, penmanship problem once and for all—literally for all.

However, as has already been shown, reading comprehension involves more than accurate decoding of symbols. It requires associative and interpretive resources that remain after the details of their acquisition are forgotten. Even skillful acts are more than reflexive responses to a stimulus. The eye blink or knee jerk is not a skill. Mowing the lawn, typing a letter, buying a garment, filling out a form, trying a law case may combine components that are purely reflexive, learned responses that have become automatic, and judgments that are more or less habitual. However, as these judgments become more rapid and sure, and the act sequences become more automatic, we call the performer and the performance skilled. Indeed, a major portion of professional practice by constant use tends towards the status of a skillful performance.

The three Rs are symbol systems that use words or other signs to stand for ideas, objects, events. Each system is non-iconic, i.e., the appearance of the word 'cat' or '75' does not resemble cats or an array of seventy-five items. For this reason instruction is needed to learn the code that ties symbol, referent and the rules together for its proper use.

Other skills are also important for school success: how to use a library, how to study, how to take examinations, how to organize one's time, how to speak effectively, how to play games. The public school is expected to produce a level of mastery that will make certain skills usable for tasks which one graduate is as likely to encounter as another. This is not easy to define, because the use of a symbolic skill is judged by varing criteria. For example, a clerk who writes a letter to the effect that "Your check for $74.00 is no good" is communicating information adequately, but what impression of the firm is being created in the mind of the reader, aside from dismay? Certain levels of discourse are expected from participants in various enterprises: that expected from the clerk in a respectable business establishment is not the same as that anticipated by college professors from their students and from each other. Social status may also demand a certain level of language usage, and language usage has been taken as a measure of intelligence. Communication, therefore, is not a sufficient criterion for linguistic adequacy, but then neither are the expectations of a particular social or economic class or profession.

The level of skill in the basics that should become a norm for schools is not clear. Minimal standards of functional literacy such as writing a business letter, reading want advertisements in the newspaper, construing a utility bill make sense and satisfy the desire of the public to ride herd on the schools. Traditionally, the mastery of the basics was justified by the needs of vocation and citizenship in a democratic society, but increasingly the citizenry is spared the trouble of acquiring high levels of skill or knowledge even if it could do so. The popular media, political parties, special interest organizations are all ready to supply answers and recommendations on demand or even in the absence of literacy. A high level of the symbolic skills cannot be justified by the need for economic, political or ideological information alone.

Before attempting to formulate an answer to this question, it might be useful to consider the aesthetic skills as a species of the symbolic skills, which are not usually listed with the three Rs. Can a case be made for their inclusion as the fourth R required in the encounter with art?

We do speak of the languages of music, the dance, drama, painting, and the like, and this might lead to grouping these languages with the language arts and mathematics as symbolic skills. But if there are such languages, their structure and use differ considerably from those mentioned. Musical notation is a set of directions for making musical sounds. Similarly, but in a far less precise fashion, there is a notation for certain dance movements. Certain devices, for example, the halo and foreshortening, are conventionalized means of conveying certain effects in painting. Nevertheless, mastery of these symbols or signs tells the beholder very little of what the work of art conveys. Whereas linguistic and mathematical symbols do just that.

Skills of aesthetic perception

Yet without some systematic way of perceiving what is portrayed in a work of art, the appreciation of it becomes literally ineffable. How to paint, sing, dance, play an instrument are skills, but not symbolic skills in the sense that the three Rs are cues to meanings. Part of the difficulty is removed if it is granted that art utilizes what has been referred to by Susanne Langer as presentational symbols as distinct from the discursive (non-iconic) symbols of reading, writing, and arithmetic. The presentational symbols are in some sense iconic — they resemble what they represent as words and numbers do not. Aesthetic forms are perceptible appearances that convey their import by those appearances.

Aesthetic perception differs from cognitive perception. The latter has as its goal the understanding of the conceptual significance of signs, and it differs from practical perception in which the symbol or sign is interpreted for its relevance to our purposes. Because we regard a painting, a musical performance or a poem as portraits of feeling, we should not have to learn to perceive what needs no translation.

Paradoxically, aesthetic perception, which should require no formal instruction, requires it almost as much, if not more, than the non-iconic symbols systems. The reasons for this have already been touched upon. The most important one is that ordinary perception is highly selective, whereas aesthetic perception is not. For example, the lights on a traffic signal are perceived as directions: stop, slow down, go. We do not, as a rule, become absorbed in the precise shades of red, green and yellow of the lights. The lonesome pine is perceived differently by the lumberman, the landscape gardener, and the casual passer by. But aesthetically, perception has to be complete: not just a yellow signal circle but the precise shade of yellow, not just a pine tree or so many board feet of lumber, but the highly complex qualities of color, shape, form, and expressiveness of feeling that trees as trees do not have.

As a result, the painting or the tree is likely to be perceived casually and for the most part unsystematically, even though the artist labored and pondered over every shape and color that reached the canvas. How to "read" a work of art or any object aesthetically, therefore, requires disciplined observation that is both analytic and holistic. The lack of such a method of analysis has restricted arts

Figure 6.2: **Making an informed aesthetic response**
Source: prepared by the author and amplified by
Professor Ronald H. Silverman, California State University,
Los Angeles

AESTHETIC PERCEPTION

First, carefully look and/or listen, note what actually exists
within an object or event, and then identify as completely as
possible the character of its

Sensory properties (qualities which can be seen, felt or heard)
- In art, identify the nature of elements such as shapes (square-round), lines (thick-thin), values (dark-light), textures (coarse-smooth), colors (bright-dull), size (large-small), space (deep-shallow), etc.
- In dance, observe body gestures (curved-angular), movements (fast-slow), space (open-contained), etc.
- In drama, observe elements such as vocal qualities (cadence, quiet-shrill), body movement (fast-slow), costumes and sets (sober-bold, realistic-abstract), etc.
- In music, identify the nature of aural qualities such as pitch (high-low), tempo (fast-slow), duration (long-short), dynamics (loud-soft), etc.

Second, respond to ways in which sensory properties are
organized within an object or event by identifying the
character of its

Formal properties (try to answer the following questions as the
work is experienced)
- To what extent is each element necessary? What is the nature of the movement (real or imagined) from one part to another thereby contributing to a sense of evolution and unity? How is the sense of unity maintained even though elements may vary, achieving unity through variety?
- Are there some elements which are more dominant than others, a hierarchy of elements? Which elements appear to be most dominant thereby contributing to the major theme? How is variety achieved in the repetition of these elements which results in thematic variation?
- How is equilibrium maintained between and among both similar and diverse parts which results in a sense of balance? What rhythmical qualities are created when mode of balance and thematic variation are combined?

Third, reflect upon both the nature of the existing sensory properties and the ways they appear to be organized and then speculate about the possible meanings of an object or event by identifying its

Expressive properties

- Aesthetic objects and events possess presentational (faces, trees, environmental sounds, familiar movements, etc.) and/or metaphorical-symbolic characteristics which evoke responses from one's storehouse of images and, when combined with sensory and formal properties, translate into pervasive qualities such as:
- Mood language — nuances of feeling describable in terms such as somber, menacing, frivolous, etc. Dynamic states — arousing a sense of tension, conflict, relaxation, etc.
  Idea and ideal language — interpretations of social or psychological events and beliefs, and/or expressions of courage, wisdom, etc.

Finally, one can also be attracted to an object or event and attempt to identify how it was created because of the significance of its

Technical Properties

- Attending to the extraordinary surface texture created by an *impasto* application of paint or the richly patterned sounds produced by the *pizzicato* plucking of violin strings are examples of reacting to the technical aspects of art forms. Knowing how something is made is often important to aesthetic perception, however, aesthetic responses and judgments can be made without such awareness if other properties are considered.

AESTHETIC CRITICISM

Historical — determining the nature and expressive intent of works of art within their historical context and in relation to school, period, style and culture.

Recreative — apprehending and relating imaginatively what the artist has expressed in a specific work.

Judicial — estimating the value of works of art in relation to other works using three criteria: degree of formal excellence, truth and significance.

education to performance training and appreciation courses that combine historical knowledge and critical judgment about works of art and artists that tell students what they ought to have perceived, but not how to do so.

Scanning

However, as was argued in Chapter 5, there is a method of analyzing aesthetic images in all media called aesthetic scanning (see Figure 6.2). Scanning is no more than perceiving systematically what the artist or nature "painted" on the surface of the object.[1] The verification of the property noted requires another act of perception — a direct comparison with the observer's report. The technical properties were included even though they are not always perceptible and, strictly speaking, not necessarily observable in the image. Their inclusion is justified pedagogically because children and adults also are interested in how effects are produced.

The expressive properties, as has been noted, are the most elusive. The scanning process works quite well with mood language, e.g., is the picture sad or glad, bold or timid, tranquil or agitated, even at the elementary grade level and elicits ready responses. The dynamic or energy language is more subtle, yet it has been found that a vocabulary describing energy states exists at the elementary grade level. The idea and ideal languages are the most difficult, albeit the traditional expectations of art are works that express such ideas and ideals. Classical art does so eminently and most representational art portrays an action, tells a story, or points to a moral. Modern art does so less obviously, yet even abstract art would reject the charge that it is meaningless.

Clearly experience plays a much greater role in perceiving the expressive properties than the sensory or the formal cues. Grant Wood's *American Gothic* is unlikely to convey its irony to a child's perception. Yet if the image does not reveal on its face some expressive quality, it loses its status as an aesthetic image, i.e., that conveys human import by virtue of its appearance.

An example of how one teacher in *The Aesthetic Eye,* Jean Neelan, explored the expressive properties is described as follows:

The following works are placed in pairs within a ringed booklet for easy comparison: Romney's *The Blue Boy*, Lawrence's *Portrait of Arthur Atherly as An Etonian*, Story's *Abraham Lincoln*, and Stuart's *George Washington*. The caption asked, "What does the print tell us about these people?" Another example of an expressive activity shows Cassat's *Summertime*,

Vuillard's *At the Seashore*, and Cézanne's *Boy Resting*, with the caption, "How do these reproductions show mood?" The final example of activities developed for expressive properties is Toulouse-Lautrec's *Dancers at the Moulin de la Galette*, Degas' *Three Dancers in Yellow Skirts*, and Mount's *The Breakdown*. (*Teacher-to-Teacher Talk,* Frances D. Hine, Gilbert A. Clark, W. Dwaine Greer, Ronald H. Silverman, eds, Aesthetic Eye Project Publications, Los Angeles, California, Nov. 1976, p. 18.)

These paintings have the advantage of being about recognizable objects. What about less obvious representations? One kindergartner, according to Gloria Larkin, in describing Picasso's *Harlequin*, thought "he looked scared ... because his face was white."[2] However, because sensory and formal properties are images of moods, energy states, and ideas, their combinations could be expected to do likewise. Hence abstract art works also elicit responses, even from young children, in terms of mood, energy, ideas, and values.

If art education is to be considered as a fourth R, aesthetic perception will have to be accompanied by aesthetic expression. The traditional drawing lessons taught pupils to delineate objects in crayon, water colors, and other media. Music lessons provided practice in singing or playing an instrument. It was also hoped that just as children express themselves in speech and writing, they could also externalize their feelings by creating art products. The emphasis on aesthetic perception need not exclude practice in expression. Classroom teachers often use the children's drawings as targets for scanning. Others have the class produce examples and variations of the sensory, formal, and expressive properties for discussion. The issue is whether there can be aesthetic education that is not primarily performance training. If not, then most of the study of literature is not aesthetic, because pupils rarely become novelists or poets.

It is argued by many art educators that aesthetic perception does not offer pupils the chance to be creative, to express themselves. This is true, but are we so sure that performance does promote creativity? How would one assess such an outcome? If arts education is to be part of the required curriculum in a school system, these questions have to be answered.

Scanning cannot supply knowledge about the history of art or the criteria for judgment used by the sophisticated critic. Scanning can do this no more than learning the three Rs can supply knowledge about the objects they signify. However, hoping to construe art or any aesthetic object without the skills of aesthetic perception is like expecting children to learn to read without learning the shapes and sounds of the letters of the alphabet.

The discussion of scanning lends plausibility to including it with the other symbolics of information as part of general education. This entry to the aesthetic image makes it plausible to speak of the fourth R. It may deglamorize art, but it gives it a place in the curriculum it has not hitherto enjoyed.

What about other skills? Should health maintenance skills, industrial skills, political skills also be included in the curriculum of general education? Certainly these skills are useful in life, but should it be the obligation of the school to develop them? If the school is a special institution with a distinctive function not shared with other institutions, it could be argued, the aforementioned skills could be developed outside of the school or by an agency other than the school on school premises. For example, the department of health might properly be charged with providing facilities for health education and training in the health maintenance skills. Industrial skills could be developed by industry or in special vocational schools. However, if the school is regarded as an all-purpose institution, then this way out is not available to it, because it would be involved directly in every activity of societal import. It makes sense for the school, as a special institution, to provide instruction sufficiently general to understand the needs and functions of other institutions, but this does not entail taking over or sharing the performance of those functions.

If the primary function of the school is to provide general education, then the symbolics of information would qualify as necessary ingredients or tools for acquiring the associative and interpretive resources through general education. Numerous other skills for replicative use may not be, albeit a community might wish to supply space and instruction to accommodate its clientele, just as it might provide space and time for eye and ear examinations during school time.

Knowledge about health and its principles, about industrial processes and their part in the social, political, and economic life of the nation does belong to general education. One cannot hope to understand the economy without some familiarity with the major types of processing that materials undergo and the technology used in these processes. Such understanding, however, is not a skill to be practised, but rather a perspective to be acquired. Since modern technology is rooted in the sciences, part of this perspective should come from the study of science. Part can come from a study of how the culture has developed, which would include the evolution of industrial technology. The use of knowledge about technology in the life of the citizen is interpretive rather than applicative or replicative.

The issue is not whether vocational training is necessary or desirable, but rather which agency should be responsible for it. To repeat a previous argument, one may choose to deny the need for general education and concentrate on training for employment. Indeed, many students and their parents would encourage schools to make this their highest priority. In a democratic society such decisions are the privilege of the electorate. In a highly technological society development of a generally educated mind may be a luxury that can either be dispensed with or postponed until after the economic goals have been achieved. However, if the decision is made in favor of general education, then its distinctive uses have to be accepted also.

Basic concepts

The interpretive use of schooling involves mastery of the cognitive and the evaluative concepts. How shall the materials of instruction be organized to help the student build the conceptual maps needed to understand the world?

With regard to the cognitive use of concepts, two types of material are available: basic sciences and developmental studies. Two other types of instruction will be examined — value exemplars and molar social problems — which together are designed to provide the materials and experience needed for the development of the valuational maps.

As Table 6.1 indicates, the basic concepts were to be derived from general science, biology, chemistry, and physics, but it also indicated that language and mathematics are not only symbolic skills, but theoretical disciplines as well. Linguistics deals with the theoretical aspects of language. The nature of quantity and quantitative relations, the deductive nature of a mathematical system and its logical properties, the basic mathematical operations and their rationale — these are the constituents of the cognitive frame needed in general education. There is a minimal set of key understandings in linguistics and mathematical theory that can be taught over a period of years, either in connection with the development of the computational and linguistic skills or a separate set of courses. The need is more marked in linguistics than in mathematics, because some of the general concepts of mathematics are already incorporated in algebra and geometry courses, whereas there is little corresponding to linguistics and information theory in the conventional language curricula.

As to the choice of sciences, two criteria may be considered: potential generality and interpretive utility. Concepts can be arranged in a logical hierarchy, with the more general subsuming the less general. In this sense, physics is more general than mechanics, the notion of an atom more so than that of a molecule, and that of a cell more general than of a type of tissue. In accordance with this principle one can limit the study of basic science to general science, physics, chemistry, and biology. Within these disciplines, however, the principle of interpretive usefulness should be the criterion, which means that only the key ideas and relations would be taught. This minimal amount, however, should be taught as science, i.e., as logically organized subject matter, with the precision required for such study.

Whether the National Science Foundation curricula in mathematics, physics, chemistry, and biology of the 1960s were really designed for interpretive use by all citizens, or whether they were primarily intended for the better preparation of the college-bound on the way to their prospective vocational careers, is not altogether clear. They seemed to promise both. When first examined, they gave the impression that students below the top quartile of the secondary-school population could not master them, and some of the preliminary testing seemed to corroborate this conjecture. However, the proponents of new curricula in mathematics and science claimed that these courses were not restricted either to the gifted or the college-bound student.

In any event, these curricula were intended for interpretive rather than applicative or replicative use. Support for this contention can be found in the following characteristics: (1) the playing down of purely descriptive accounts of physical phenomena and technological application of principles, (2) emphasis on key ideas, and (3) stress on methods of inquiry by which the sciences achieved their current status. Even the laboratory work was not intended to develop manipulative skill but designed to help the student appreciate the way in which science and technology interplay, and, above all, to provide firsthand experience of what happens when one uses the hypothetico-deductive-experimental method.

One might argue that this kind of science teaching has as its aim the applicative use of science, but unless supplemented by a good deal of detailed, advanced work in a given field, such study will remain interpretive. It may not be used to advance work in science or even to use science to solve life problems. It may, however, be the very best way for the citizen to grasp the import of science for life and its problems.

Some science teachers may not share this conception of science teaching. The interpretive use of science may seem to smack of superficiality and soft pedagogy. There is also the problem of convincing the student that the sciences being studied should be for interpretation rather than for immediate application. To get some notion of how the uses of science are perceived by the college student, about three hundred undergraduates at a large state university were asked to rank seven uses of science: cognitive, theoretical, vocational, practical, recreational, methodological, and adjustative.

One-half of the students ranked in first or second place the adjustative use of science, which was defined on the questionnaire as "having sufficient knowledge to feel at home in a world where science is important." However, more than 40 per cent put into first or second place the practical use (putting anti-freeze in your car, washing synthetic fabrics, and so on), what this book calls the applicative use of science.

By rating the adjustative role of science so highly, these students affirmed the importance of interpreting the world scientifically. Yet only 18 per cent assigned the cognitive use of science first or second place. (The cognitive use was defined as "being able to read scientific books and articles with understanding.") How they expected to use science for interpretation without reading scientific materials is not easy to understand. As a matter of fact, twice as many students placed the theoretical use of science (enjoying a knowledge of science for its own sake; obtaining information to satisfy curiosity) in first and second place as ranked the reading of scientific books and articles with understanding in these positions. Again, one wonders how they plan to "do" science or "enjoy" science without reading scientific materials, because to read such materials one needs to have learned the ideas and language of science.

Apparently it was not clear to these respondents that to feel at home in a world where science is important means a mastery of the key concepts of the basic sciences, and mastery is not to be confused with mere familiarity. The interpretive use of science involves more than passing familiarity with and diffuse admiration for science. On the contrary, interpretation calls for a highly precise use of concepts, although not in a replicative or applicative way.

Thus, even among many college students the impression probably persists that the study of science is justified by its usefulness in dealing with such individual, everyday technological problems as coping with the family automobile and household appliances. It cannot be denied that a good course in physics helps make the workings of these appliances more intelligible (knowledge about our technology helps even more), but it does not necessarily help one fix a broken pump or the transmission system of an automobile. Between the understanding and the doing lies a layer of rules and tools, know-how and skills. When this layer becomes thick and complicated, as it does in a highly developed technology, science as such cannot be used by the layman to fix automobiles and water faucets. For this reason, our society is as dependent on the technician as it is on the scientist: the layman can no more take on the duties of either at a moment's notice, than he can quickly take on the role of a modern soldier. Hence the stress on the importance of differentiating between the applicative and the interpretive uses of science. Science in general education cannot be justified on the grounds that it will help the individual operate and repair machinery, on the one hand, or that he will use it in his vocation, on the other. It is on the grounds of interpretation, on the need we all have to understand our world and society, that the justification must be based.

When science is used interpretively, we ask that it help us think and discourse about such questions as the following: What is it? How is this related to other things? What consequences can I expect from it? How did it come to be what it is? What laws describe the way it behaves? How does its behavior correlate with the behavior of certain other things? We are asking for information that will allow us to place the object of our inquiry into a cognitive or knowledge perspective.

Examining these questions more closely, one sees that some of them ask for classificatory information: To what class of objects does a thing belong? Is this class a subclass of a larger class? For example, is the cancer problem to be classified as a problem of biology, chemistry or as a subtopic of physics? Is it an infection? Is it a type of cell growth? Does it belong to the group of diseases caused by viruses? By tissue injuries? In the early stages of inquiry, definitions are needed to help sort out whatever information one happens to have about infectious diseases, the effects of radiation on cell growth, and so on. Later, as one becomes more familiar with the matter, one realizes that the classification problem has not yet been solved. Indeed, if it could be determined to what group of diseases cancer belonged, the next steps would be much clearer. Inquiry is oriented by classification, and by refining classification knowledge is rendered more precise.

In addition to classification questions, there are questions about causal relations and relations of covariation. What causes what and what varies with what are the two most important questions we can ask. The greater the number of items that can be tied together in a logical rational net, the better orientation is, and the more revealing is the perspective. This net of relations is woven by the basic and the developmental sciences. One outcome of general education should be the formation of such a categorial or conceptual net.

Developmental studies

Not all sciences are basic. Some serve not so much to organize knowledge as to sustain the social order. Agriculture, medicine, technology, and national defense are examples. So are political science, jurisprudence, economics, and administration; they are concerned with the proper functioning of society as a whole. Furthermore, the notion of basic concepts so clear in the physical sciences — because there is already a strong consensus as to what they are — is not at all clear in the social sciences or the professional studies that may employ the concepts of a number of sciences. When it comes to the interpretive resources needed to understand life in a modern society, there is still far to go after having acquired the basic concepts of physics, chemistry, and biology. There will still be a host of phenomena in the physical world that will be difficult to interpret, e.g., the development of the cosmos in general and in particular the peculiarities of our own planet. As to the social, moral, religious, economic aspects of life on this planet, the mastery of the basic concepts of three physical sciences and even general science courses will leave many of these territories as murky as before.

Because the curriculum of general education has to forego the hope of teaching all the subjects needed for interpretive purposes, it may be advisable to consider a trio of developmental studies. These are cognitive maps that organize wide arrays of diverse concepts. They are indicated in Figure 6.1, as Development of the Cosmos, Development of Institutions, and Development of the Culture.[3]

Cosmos — Developmental Studies I

It is generally agreed that the cosmos has a history. The planetary system as a whole, and indeed the entire galactic system, are believed to have emerged into their present form as a result of previous events. Astronomy and geology, for example, give accounts of these developments. However, these sciences contain much more than theories of development. The theories, after all, are attempts to account for basic data, such as the movements of planets and eclipses and differences in the composition of various layers of the earth. Much of the content of these sciences deals with the results of observation, classification, methods of observation, and tools of observation and measurement.

Few would deny the importance of these sciences for general education and the desirability of studying them systematically, if it were possible to do so. Yet, if a choice must be made, and if one asks what aspects of astronomy and geology are most useful for interpretive use, it is to the general theories of how the earth and celestial systems came to have their present characteristics and how scientists have developed the means for securing and interpreting their data that one would turn for an answer.

The problem, of course, is how to select the topics and materials with which these outcomes can be achieved. How much astronomy and geology must the pupil do in order to construct the cognitive map needed to interpret the import of celestial and terrestrial phenomena? How much does one need even to understand the "story" of the heavens and the earth?

At this stage of curriculum construction, a partnership between the educators and the astronomer or the geologist (unless both roles are happily combined in one person) is imperative. The educator is needed because astronomers, quite properly, want astronomy taught for the purpose of doing astronomy. The educator is needed to take account of the difference between doing astronomy and using astronomy for interpretation. The astronomer is needed because whatever is taught should, first of all, be "good" astronomy, and only the professional astronomer is qualified to make this judgment.

Similar considerations can be adduced for constructing the developmental accounts of living things, including man. However, a whole group of sciences will have to be drawn upon for this account, so the extent of collaboration and the number of decisions are enormously increased. In addition to biology (which is to be studied separately), there are paleontology (the study of fossils), zoology, botany, climatology, various ecologies, and physical anthropology, to mention only a few of the sciences that deal with the development of living things. The same distinction between doing these sciences and using them to develop cognitive interpretive maps must be made; there are the same problems of selecting materials and arranging them for instruction as were discussed in relation to astronomy and geology.

Nevertheless, it is a selective rather than originative task. Each of the sciences mentioned does have a developmental aspect. Each, after all, does try to reconstruct the past. Each, in other words, includes a theory about how this reconstruction should be undertaken.

Institutions — Developmental Studies II

The second segment of the developmental studies reconstructs the development of the family, church, economic systems, governmental systems, laws, and other institutions devised by men to order and nurture their societies.

The materials for this strand of the developmental studies are drawn from anthropology, sociology, economic and political history, as well as the history of jurisprudence. The focus of this segment is the role of social institutions in social change, and how social institutions develop under the stress of change in other sectors of human life.

Courses in political science, sociology, anthropology, and economics are only infrequently found in the secondary curriculum, and there is little prospect that they all can be introduced as separate subjects. The arguments cited in the case of the sciences having to do with the evolution of the earth and life can also be applied here. On the one hand, there is a crying need for the kind of knowledge embodied in these disciplines; on the other, there is no viable way of introducing all of them into the curriculum as separate subjects for systematic study.

The family, church, government, economic system, and school are among the key social arrangements in our life. Their functions determine much of what we do and are. For individuals to orient their own, and the community's problems with respect to these institutions is no small part of general education. Development Studies II undertakes to trace the development of such instruction in order to show how and why one form succeeded another, how and why the functions were modified, how and why social stress was manifested in these shifts of function.

The *how* and *why* indicate the role of the social sciences as a source of the materials, because the explanatory generalizations necessarily have to come from them. Here again the curriculum-maker is calling for a vast collaborative enterprise. Again, it is a selective rather than an originating task. Much has already been done in these directions, but a clever experiment here and a project there do not make a curriculum. It is for agreement on a unifying set of themes that one can look to the leaders in social science education. Given consensus on the themes, diverse choices of materials will not destroy it.

In this connection, it may be noted that the Developmental Studies II displace the current courses in history in the curriculum (as well as geography, and social studies), a point that will hardly elicit applause from the historians. Because historians and teachers of history have been among the most adamant and vocal foes of the absorption of their subject into an area called "social studies," some further defense of the omission of the conventional courses in history as a high school subject is required.

One purpose of history is to provide interpretive frames for understanding current social problems. We often say that to understand this or that problem, it is only necessary to recite its history. For example, to explain the current school calendar, one needs to recall the need for children's help on the farm during the summer months. Why, then, do not the conventional courses in history serve as interpretive resources *par excellence*?

From the remnants of what adults can remember about the American Revolution or the Civil War, what is available for interpreting current social problems, such as taxation policy? Not much unless that course went into the economic and political problems of the eighteenth century in Europe. If it did, then it would be using generalizations from economics and political science, social psychology, and much else.[4]

All of this seems to indicate that in order to make the study of history anything more than a bare chronology of names, dates, and places, the pupil should first be grounded in the social sciences. The hope that the basic concepts of the social sciences will be learned as a result of studying history seems poorly founded, especially if one relies on the commonly used textbooks in high school history.

It may be unreasonable to expect history to carry the pedagogical burden of providing understandings in the multiplicity of disciplines mentioned above. This is one reason for urging something like developmental studies as a way of organizing materials for secondary-school instruction. It does not dispense with historians, but it does call for greater participation by historians of science, economics, politics, sociology, and technology in the preparation of curricular materials.

Culture — Developmental Studies III

The development of the cosmos and human institutions goes a long way toward filling in the maps for cognitive interpretation. They provide concepts, generalizations, and causal sequences into which many life situations can be fitted for interpretation.

There are, however, still other elements needed for our cognitive maps. They are the ideas and the artifacts by which human needs are expressed and fulfilled. The press is a social institution, but the printing press was the artifact that made the press the power it is. Art, literature, philosophy, religion, technology, and the development of the sciences themselves are phenomena that need to be understood.

Once more, the difference between being artistic, religious, inventive, literary, or scientific and knowing about these activities must be reiterated. While knowledge about art or religion may or may not affect our attitudes and behavior, it is not the same as *doing* these things. Our judgment may or may not coincide with our preferences. It is in the strand of the curriculum called "exemplars" that these two components of value experience are brought together.

Whenever we try to combine knowledge in a subject with knowledge about it, one or the other suffers. Trying to understand the role of chemistry in the development of the culture, for example, is bound to take time from studying chemical phenomena and theory.

Hence, something like cultural history or the history of culture is needed to complete the cognitive map. Just as social institutions affect our thought and action, so do the ideologies and technologies of the culture. Developmental Studies III are the developmental accounts of human culture, including its sciences, technologies, art, literature, systems of ideas, and religions.

Naturally, there will be overlapping among the contents of the three types of developmental studies. This is not bad, provided the same materials occur in different contexts. The problem is not duplication as such, but rather to strike a viable balance between keeping together in a course of study the elements that go together in the phenomena, on the one hand, and creating a pedagogical hash, on the other. A pedagogical hash results whenever one undertakes to talk about everything at once or in the same course. Integration of topics reaches a point of diminishing returns when details obscure structure. The three strands of developmental study, therefore, integrate by distinguishing among the types of phenomena grouped for study. Furthermore, the preparation of materials for any one of these developmental strands is difficult enough without asking for the collaboration of persons competent in all three.

Again, it must be noted that philosophy and the intellectual content of religion, as well as the history of the arts and sciences, can be taught in separate courses, and it should go without further repetition that, given sufficient time, one might choose to study these matters systematically in separate courses. But there is no sufficiency of time, and the interpretive frame provided by development of our most human of human accomplishments is the most important of all interpretive frames.

Knowledge *about* the development of the various strands of the culture can do no more than draw a cognitive map in very broad outline, keeping in mind that the developmental strands represent what seems to be the best alternative to ignoring such development altogether, or having no map at all. It places a high premium on the selection of the materials to be included and their organization so that they are studied as processes of cognitive development and not as random collections of phenomena.

Yet even if well designed and executed, these developmental strands plus the basic concept of the sciences, plus the skills of symbolics still leave open the formation of norms for judgment and appreciation. Science, so to speak, argues that X is true because it meets the requirements of scientific criteria or because it fits into a developmental schema backed by historical evidence. What justifies saying that X is good and ought to be desired? The latter question is commonly studied in the normative disciplines: ethics, value theory, criticism in the arts — where norms in the various value domains are systematically argued.

These questions pertain to the justification of preference and tastes; they do not deal directly with how the preferences are formed in the first place. The latter query pushes us into the maze of conditionings and pressures that begin with birth and persist to the last day of life. One would like to think of general education exerting an influence on both the formation of preferences and their justification. Once more, the limitation of time prevents the school, especially the public school, from including in its curriculum the vast array of the valuative disciplines that scholarship has produced. Even programs of liberal studies at the collegiate level do not guarantee an adequate sampling of the normative issues in the several value domains.

This age-old war between heart and head has its pedagogical counterpart in the circumstance that two distinct types of learning are involved in value education. Tastes and dispositions are, in the first instance, products of conditioning that takes place in the home, in the streets, and, to a lesser extent, in the school. The pupil spends only a few hours a day in school, and the school does not have the machinery to reinforce systematically anything save scholastic achievement and a respect for the accepted *mores* of the school community. The school can, at best, modify tastes already formed. The young pupil's existing preferences and attitudes do not sample the totality of value possibilities very well, either with respect to depth or range. In every value domain — social, recreational, civic, moral, intellectual, aesthetic, and religious — there are levels of preference. In the informal environment, the pupil has probably not encountered the level of preference exhibited by value experts. Just as one expects the school to bring the expert's thought to bear upon the pupil's inexpert knowledge, so it is reasonable for the school to bring the expert's values to bear upon the pupil's rudimentary taste.

Theoretically, it is interesting and important to ask whether there are or can be objective value standards, standards of right and wrong, good and evil, the beautiful and the ugly. Educationally, however, especially at the secondary level, there is only one practical solution to this problem: to rely on the experts in these fields as the school relies on experts in other fields. The school does not determine what is *good* chemistry, and it does not determine what is *good* literature or art. "Good" means what scholars who have devoted their professional lives to the study of these domains have agreed is good. Truth here is not simply consensus, but rather the consensus of persons qualified to have expert opinions.

Where these experts do not agree, the school can only proceed on the principle that the major alternatives deserve to be presented. Expert disagreement does not license the ignorant or change the nature of expertness. On the contrary, this kind of disagreement is the best incitement to inquiry into grounds of disagreement, an important first step to becoming an expert on one's own account. There is enough agreement among the experts to supply more than enough material for any secondary-school curriculum.

Who are the value experts? Presumably, those men and women who have experienced and reflected upon what gives the highest satisfaction in each value domain. It is to the great artists, writers, philosophers, and saints that we look for wisdom. Because the pupil cannot replicate the expert's life directly, the school has recourse to the reports of value experts, the connoisseurs of life. These reports, in the form of works of art, systems of philosophy, and religions, present pupils with an array of possibilities far richer and far more subtle than they could ever imagine.

Exemplars

These great works represent value affirmations that integrated and vividly expressed the character of the successive epochs in our history. Their influence reaches into the present. One may loosely call these value exemplars *classics*, not only because they have been admired and preferred by generations of experts, but also because they furnish the experts with the criteria for judging them *excellent*. Classics in any field are not only highly satisfactory on their own account, but the source of norms of *proper* satisfaction as well. Therein lies their pedagogical value, for in learning to appreciate them, the pupil not only likes what the connoisseur likes, but is at the same time exposed to the source of the criteria that the connoisseur has used to justify the liking.

Once more it becomes necessary to choose among the enormous resources of the literature on values and even among the classical examples in the fields of philosophy, religion, literature and the other arts. To a considerable extent the selection of exemplars from these fields is limited by the technical requirements of these fields. Highly technical works in philosophy and religion, for example, are probably not suitable for grades 7–12. Literature is already represented in the curriculum, but usually in the form of selections from various periods. The performing arts are for the most part to be found among the electives.

Furthermore, if the arts are to be made part of the required curriculum, there has to be developed a mode of teaching them for aesthetic perception and appreciation rather than for the development of performance skills. Finally, an exemplar, if it is to serve as the representative of an important phase of the culture it represents, must be studied over a sufficient length of time to affect the student's perception, so that he or she begins to see the world through the eyes and ears of the exemplar. This means that the list of exemplars will be relatively small. All of which places a great premium on the selection process.

By way of concluding the treatment of exemplars, one can return to the notion of evaluative maps. They determine the way we order our preferences, just as cognitive maps fashion the way we classify and interpret our knowledge. There are, to be sure, cognitive elements in judgments of value, just as there are in judgments of fact. Nevertheless, our operations in the value field are so circumscribed by conditionings that education faces a harder task in changing values than in changing beliefs. Accordingly, one component of value education is a kind of value reconditioning; another component is the justification for one preference rather than another. Both components are brought into play by the use of value models as displayed in exemplars from the arts.

Exemplars do not exhaust the requirements of value education. There remains the act of choice itself, especially when it entails the interplay of many values in many dimensions, as it does in what may be social or molar problem solving, which takes us into the citizen's use of knowledge and schooling.

CHAPTER 7

The citizen's use of schooling

Many schemes for citizenship education have been recommended and not a few have been tried. The most familiar is the study of the Declaration of Independence, the Constitution, the machinery of the government at the national, state, and local levels. Sometimes the history of the state's governmental institutions has been mandatory in the civics course.

Another mode of citizenship education required students to act out the roles of the citizen in arriving at decisions on public issues. Debates were one form of this approach. Another was to transform the classroom into a community in which issues were raised, discussed, and decided. Still another was to study actual community issues. Perhaps the oldest method was to rely on the study of selected classics to inculcate ideals of citizenship and to furnish eloquent defenses for them. Cicero's orations would be an example, as would the stories of patriotism as reported by Homer and other famous poets and dramatists.

I am not acquainted with research studies that definitively decide for or against these methods, but certain deficiencies in each of them have been noted, often as grounds for suggesting alternative approaches. Roughly, the difficulties fall into a few categories. The most common is that theoretical materials have no direct effect on behavior, because their motivational magnetism is weak. More particularly there is the objection or recognition that the adult citizen has motives that often are stronger than the ideals of civic virtue; that actions contrary to the spirit of these ideals are common enough to mistrust their influence.

Less common, but perhaps even more cogent, is the fact that citizenship in a modern society, especially in a democratic one, calls for a degree of understanding the issues on which the citizen is expected to make judgments that can no longer be a realistic goal for all but specialists in economics, government, and information analysis. The reasons for this have already been discussed at several points, but they come to this: the complexity of modern life, the high level of technology entailed by virtually all transactions in which the citizen participates, and the deluge of information and propaganda all conspire to bewilder even the well-intentioned and intelligent citizen.

The school as a community

Neither in knowledge nor feeling does the urbanized, mechanized city of the twentieth century enjoy the homogeneity of the earlier and smaller American community. It is not surprising that educators saw the problem in the early years of the century as a restoration of the face-to-face controls of the small, semi-rural community. Because they could not reverse time, it seemed plausible for them to regard the school as the instrument by which, as John Dewey put it, the city could be provided with a simplified, balanced, and purified environment, that is, the ideal community.[1]

In such a community, it was argued, pupils would be motivated to share their cognitions and feelings about the common good. *Ergo*, an activity curriculum should replace the highly symbolic and verbal one.

Although Dewey was the philosophical ancestor of the activity curriculum and the problem-solving style of teaching, the man who probably had the most to do with bringing this method of teaching into the classroom was William Heard Kilpatrick.

By 1916 he had the largest enrollment of any teacher at Columbia Teachers College. Hailed as the "million dollar professor" because his students had paid over a million dollars in fees to the University, it is estimated that he had 35,000 students, mostly from the ranks of classroom teachers, school principals, and social workers. The influence of Kilpatrick was extended by his writings, especially by one article in particular, "The Project Method".[2]

The notion that the school should become a community in which the pupil could directly practise being a citizen, i.e., have a voice in making at least some decisions about the conduct of the school, tries to supplement cognitive resources with direct political experience. This approach has many variations, but two deserve special consideration. One is to stress the variety of ideologies and value systems in the culture and to have the students confront this diversity with attempts to find common ground. The other is to include in the curriculum a strand called "molar problem solving." The aim of the first approach is to cultivate tolerance for ideological differences and to develop a community of feeling and ideation. Central to this approach is the abandonment or denial of transcendent value systems that claim precedence over cultural differences of outlook and interest.

There is a whole genre of literature that stresses the theory that all value commitments and social theories are the products of cultural pressures by power groups, i.e., the thesis of Thrasymachus in Plato's *Republic*, viz., that justice is the interest of the stronger. Accepting this diversity as inevitable, the role of education is to encourage the habits and techniques of discovering enough commonality of interest to render political action possible.

As many readers have already suspected, these issues stir up centuries of philosophical literature trying to determine the rational grounds for belief in objective standards of value in general, and of moral value in particular. The uses of such literature are varied — replicative for the undergraduate preparing for an exam in a philosophy course, applicative for the professor giving the course, associative for most, and interpretive for the educated mind. A recent book by Bernard Williams[3] reviews anew the issue between the objectivists, who argue that there are and must be standards of right and wrong that all rational human beings acknowledge, and those who like Williams reject the possibility of such objectivity.

Let us suppose the graduate of the secondary school, well on the road to becoming educated, has acquired the symbolic skills, the concepts of the basic sciences, and the cognitive-evaluative maps promised by the developmental studies and exemplars. What in the curriculum gives promise that the graduate can now cope with the problems of living in a democratic society or even understanding them? Granted these ingredients make such a promise plausible, what in the school experience makes it more than mere conjecture? What in the school curriculum corresponds to such uses of schooling in life?

The answer given in this essay is the strand called molar problem solving.

Molar problem solving

The argument for this strand is that formal study of the sciences, the developmental strands, and even the exemplars were resources *with* which to think and appreciate. They did not guarantee that these resources would be so used. Hence some experience with typical problem-solving situations was indicated. Some of these could be actual difficulties encountered by students. Early adolescence certainly does not lack for problems, and while they are not yet the problems facing the adult citizen, they are not independent of them. After all, what to do with youth is a perennial social, economic, moral and political problem.

However, my colleagues and I were reluctant to recommend converting the school into a living, breathing, debating hive of problem-solving activity as Kilpatrick counseled.[4] For one thing, would such a community manage to probe the arts and sciences sufficiently and with enough variety to build the moral, intellectual, and aesthetic resources that make up the educated mind — the allusionary base — for associative and interpretive uses of schooling? Such cognitive and appreciative insights as might be gained would not be systematic or necessarily representative of the arts and sciences.

Life presents us with predicaments from which we try to extricate ourselves by habit, luck, trial and error, and, on occasion, by thinking. Presumably the distinctive contribution of the school is to convert at least the more generic predicaments into problems that become amenable to Dewey's complete act of thought. The amount of systematic thinking demanded by modern life from the ordinary citizen in his non-vocational roles is probably overestimated. For as a culture becomes more and more complicated, more and more dependent on sophisticated technology, the amount of individual thinking the system can wait for is severely limited. More and more citizens have to use this technology without understanding what makes it work. The increased demand for logical creative thought by the few (the experts) is accompanied by the decreased need of such thought by the many (the consumers). If ordinary everyday life in a modern society is the standard, schooling for thinking or problem solving is becoming less necessary rather than more. Apparently the unexamined life is very much worth living. What, then, does make rational life worth the trouble? For the bright and energetic, problem solving as a professional activity can be very rewarding — money, self-esteem, social success can be rewarding indeed. For the many, self-cultivation — what has been referred to as the educated mind and taste — makes sense only if it enhances the quality of life in the several value domains; and, only if such enhancement cannot be bought ready made from the long list of how-to books.

The citizen confronts predicaments after the fashion of someone in a maze. Investigation, after fruitless trial and error, discloses alternative routes, but each may have blocks and alternatives of its own. Like the experimental rat, one can work a way out by trial and error, or rehearse some previously used solutions. Each is easier than discerning the design of the maze as a whole. If such a maze is envisioned as numerous paths lying on different planes, drawn to different scales of measurement, one begins to approximate the complexity and multilateral dimensions of a problem such as taxation or foreign trade. Such problems are best designated as "molar."

Not all problems are equally useful for pedagogical purposes. Multi-dimensional ones, e.g., those of public policy, are preferable because they require some preliminary associative and interpretive thinking before a solution is attempted. One of these steps is making a judgment about the sort of data and knowledge that are relevant to the situation. It is to make this step possible and fruitful that the cognitive and evaluative maps are developed in general education. For it is the residual content of the basic sciences, exemplars, and the developmental studies that should provide the resources for these judgments of relevance.

What shape should the molar problem solving take for instruction? Unless it becomes the design for the entire curriculum, it must stand as one strand along with the four others. Few rather than many problems are in order because (1) the objective is not to solve all or most of the current social problems, but rather to become accustomed to thinking about them systematically, (2) the complexity of these problems makes heavy demands on time, and (3) teachers cannot possibly become expert on a wide range of such problems. The aim of the molar problems strand is to test the efficacy of the other strands rather than to provide the student with solutions.

The practice needed takes the form of (1) clarifying the statement of the problem, (2) exploring its ramifications, (3) making estimates about relevant information and theory, (4) exploring logical, psychological, and societal causes for disagreement, and (5) formulating solutions and criticizing them.

In addition to the logical operations connected with problem solving, there is a spate of emotional, personal, and ideological factors. These often are greater obstacles to problem solving than the methodological ones. The student movements of the 1960s and 1970s, the protests against the war in Vietnam, the battles for women's rights, minority rights, and civil rights in general generated acrimony that could not be dissolved by appeals to reasonableness. There needs to be some sort of group therapy that enables participants to examine and perhaps introject the attitudes of others. Such psychological devices prevent the premature hardening of positions and soften those already formed.[5]

The subsequent decades witnessed massive social movements in which the socio-psychological factors figured more prominently than the cognitive ones.[6]

A common theme in the 1960s was that schools socialized children into accepting the unequal conditions in the prevailing society; that the dominant social classes used the schools to preserve that dominance. In the early 1970s a literature on educational alternatives flourished, including numerous proposals for free schools and no schools.[7]

If to these complications are added the rise of theories of knowledge that render all value judgments relative to forces operating in the culture rather than outcomes of rational inquiry, and if rational inquiry is itself reduced to personal and hermeneutical interpretation, it is clear that value education in the school curriculum is no longer to be regarded as a simplified version of the project method of teaching, or as a standard set of topics and literatures.[8]

However, if the commitment to the idea of an educated mind has any useful meaning, it must include the ability to approach these problems with the images, skills, and concepts of the arts and sciences. To those who argue that such faith is itself irrational, this notion of the educated mind makes no sense, but it would be difficult to discern what education would make sense in a nonsensical world. The argument that relating rather than thinking is the proper solution converts the school into a mental clinic to prevent or cure cognitive addiction.

This is not to deny that in many aspects of social life it is power in one form or another wielded by those who have it over those who don't that counts rather than principles in the name of which the power is exercised. And there is no need to rehearse the consequences of such views for action. The counter move is to define *licit* power with which to confront the illicit brand. The grounds for defining the licit use of power range from Hegel's dialectic as interpreted by Marx to an emotional identification with the feelings of the masses, individually or collectively. As between the school indoctrinating youth in the values and beliefs of this or that social class or in the consensus of the learned, the latter is preferable because in a clash between classes how can a choice between them be justified on grounds other than on their truth claims? And truth can be claimed on rational grounds only if supported by arguments that have been shaped and tested by the institutions devoted to scholarship. Once the public school abandons this criterion, it is at the mercy of political power exercised directly by force or indirectly through the ballot box. The will of the government, however expressed, is no more justified rationally than the quality of evidence and principle adduced for it. Sooner or later the source of that evidence becomes the issue, whether it is raised on a national scale or in a problem-solving activity in the classroom.

Because the issue is complicated and crucial, the notion of the school as a community is a debatable metaphor. For this reason, the molar problem strand of the curriculum is intended to serve only as a sample of how schooling can be used in adult life in its problem-solving mode rather than as a slice of that life. It is a test-run, so to speak, of how the learnings in the other strands of the curriculum — symbolics of information, concepts, developmental studies, and exemplars — are used in confronting the predicaments of adult life.

Perhaps even this claim oversimplifies the actual conditions under which the citizen confronts the predicaments of the social order. In a modern society there are many obstacles to converting predicaments into intellectual problems.

Judgments of truth

In socio-political life the citizen confronts predicaments through the lenses of the media. Even very personal situations have to be translated into the ways institutions view them. Health care, to take a very personal situation, has to be translated into the professional *mores* and procedures of medical practice. Diagnosis and treatment of the illness is governed by the "state of the art" medicine, but the actual services are dispensed in accordance with health-care schemes and administrative devices that can be far more complicated than the diseases to be treated.

Instead of paying a standard fee to a physician, diagnosis and treatment can become a highly complicated series of appointments with a half-dozen departments and cadres of personnel in a hospital or clinic, let alone finding a parking space. How fees are paid out of a complex of benefits too complicated to describe, let alone understand, is a puzzle for the ordinary citizen. There being little hope of understanding the *mélange* of agencies, rules, and jurisdictions, the citizen learns the routines and practises them by rote.

Even the well intentioned and normally intelligent citizen can barely make out the meaning and import of legislation at the local, county, state, and federal levels. The net impact of reading dutifully about such legislation, and listening to radio and television is a vague sense of import drifting through clouds of committees, councils, court rooms, and legislative bodies. The citizens hear and read interpretations of these procedures, but their real meaning becomes clear only when an official missive arrives containing a bill or a warning of one sort or another.

As for understanding economic problems, on what must the well-intentioned citizen depend? An educated citizen may understand the basic concepts of economics, but the concepts of economics are of little help, if economists construe the same data to mean X will and will not happen. Furthermore, few, if any, economic problems are local. It is a cliché that economic situations are likely to be global in their causes and ramifications. So, while the citizen is expected to understand and even legislate on these problems, the ability to understand them is constantly diminishing.

This situation can be dealt with in several ways. (1) Citizens may stop trying to interpret socio-economic-political problems altogether. They can swim with the stream and scream only when it threatens to drown them in unwanted consequences. (2) They can try to absorb what the media show and tell and make a choice among the possibilities presented. (3) They can purchase brokerage services. (4) They can, if they have benefited from general education, site the contingencies of life in a democratic society on the associative and cognitive maps that have become part of their allusionary base.

Economics, history, political science, philosophy proffer such maps. Discussion and analysis need not issue in unequivocal conclusions, but they can clarify options and appraise their possible consequences. These maps are lenses or stencils through which the episodic reports of the media can be examined and their consistency or lack of it assessed. Hypotheses can be formulated, criticized, and possibly tested, if not in action, then in imaginary scenarios.

These intellectual maneuvers may satisfy the need for clarification and consistency, but why are they so lacking in persuasive power that more often than not they lead not to decision but to further discussion?

Suppose a group is considering a prospective change in the income tax laws. The arguments grounded in economic and political theory have been stated and their consequences projected. If A decides the passage of the legislation would increase his taxes and B concludes that it would reduce hers, what should their decisions be? And which principles would be summoned to justify that choice? If they choose their own advantage, would it be because it followed from their economic/political theories or would it be simple selfishness? Or would it be a happy coincidence of both?

Suppose A decides to support the legislation (and increase his taxes), whereas B opposes it even though it would reduce her tax bill. Would this be evidence for their economic and political wisdom or for their credibility? It certainly would indicate loyalty to principles that transcend personal advantage. But how can this happen? After all, the theory that an economy based on greed and need is supposed to be true applies not only to economic principles but to psychological ones as well. That A should support the measure even though it is not profitable for him to do so, therefore, is a paradox indeed. Does *faith* in Adam Smith's Invisible Hand have room for a "higher selfishness?" Or are such paradoxes simply logical mistakes? Yet those paradoxes are not only possible but testify to the existence and potency of value norms that contravene the universality of selfishness in human motivation. It was this very possibility of acting on a principle contrary to inclination on which Kant founded his argument for the possibility of a moral law.

Judgments of credibility

Fideistic considerations of this sort enter into the citizen's thinking about social and economic policy. Deciding and voting go beyond the logical criteria of truth and practical efficiency. The weighing of evidence needed for warranted assertion is not enough for warranted commitment. To find evidence freed of all personal and circumstantial factors is itself difficult — some would say impossible — precisely because personal and circumstantial factors necessarily become part of the data base. The Complete Act of Thought as a design for social/political/economic problem solving breaks down when these factors can neither be eliminated nor neutralized. For the citizen in a complex society they can rarely, if ever, be wholly eliminated. Hence the citizen resorts to other criteria for judgment, viz., the criteria of credibility.

Consider the following assertions:

1 Candidate A or candidate A's proposal is sound because *it* will produce the results A promises, and I like or dislike the results.
2 Candidate A's proposal is made in good faith because A does not stand to profit from it.
3 A stands to profit from passage of his proposal.

The intelligent, well-meaning citizen has reason to favor A's proposal on objective grounds (1) if he/she knows and can evaluate these grounds, but suppose one cannot do so, then either (2) or (3) or no judgment at all follows.

Why does credibility depend so heavily on A's willingness to act contrary to self interest? Clearly because to do so consciously and deliberately connotes a loyalty to a principle "higher" than the "natural" propensity to selfishness. It heightens the probability that A is considering the general welfare rather than A's alone.

Discussion of issues in the media provides ample evidence of the importance of credibility in political life. It would be strange — indeed, incredible — for candidates seeking office to declare that their election would benefit themselves and their friends as well as the voters. When the head of a giant corporation suggested that what is good for General Motors is good for the country, the citizenry was mildly shocked. Was the shock the result of doubting the truth of the claim or the reaction to the impropriety of uttering it? Such a public utterance increased the credibility of the head of General Motors — he was sincere in his belief, and demonstrated considerable courage in uttering it. Was the principle true? Relevant evidence was available to test it — presumably correlations between the company's profits and the measures of the national economy could provide it. Was the utterance ungraciously received because it was known to be untrue or because the speaker was not credible? Or was it disapproval of unseemly pride?

Let us suppose, however, that the General Motors claim is generalized as a conclusion from arguments in favor of a free market economy as the cure for all social ills. Would this make it less distasteful? Not to the workers displaced by more "efficient" means of production. Certainly not by labor unions whose members are likely to bear the immediate consequences of strict exercise of a free market economy. Granted that these demurrers are themselves motivated by self-concern, why is it that *laissez faire* economics has always disturbed the sensibilities of many segments of society, even among those who benefited from it? Why has so much public benevolence of the very wealthy captains of industry been attributed to a bad conscience, if it were not for the suspicion that the fortunes were accumulated by the exploitation of those whose need prevented their resistance? But why is such exploitation bad? If it is necessary for the maximization of productivity, why cavil at the price? Surely benevolent charity by those who profit from such a system should serve to allay sentimentalism and what has been called the sentimentality of those who persist in mixing up notions of profit and propriety, the "wretched" poor with the "deserving" poor.

A similar argument can be mounted between the advocates of a strong defense for the nation and those who purport to place human values above national ones. Both views are rooted in a theory of the state and the state of mankind. Both claim to be defending the benefit of all, but neither side trusts the motives of the other.

Value norms

The source of these anomalies is not hard to locate. It is the pool of ideals and values that intrudes into the consideration of the public good. Each society and each social stratum lives by images of the good that give content to their concepts of the good. These concepts, in turn, are used as criteria for judgment in all departments in life, yet on positivistic criteria, these norms and ideals seem to float irrelevantly above reality rather than constituting it. Nevertheless, this apparent insubstantiality does not diminish their potency.

Pupils do not wait for formal schooling to acquire norms of conduct and feeling, but schooling is expected to bring the fruits of scholarship to evaluating and refining these norms. Philosophy is supposed to clarify and purify tribal beliefs and customs. The arts, especially literature, portray these ideals in vivid form, creating images that allow them to be perceived as well as conjured up for thought. This is what is meant by the educated mind and educated imagination as distinguished from the thoughts and images ground in by routine participation in the life of the group.

All forms of knowledge and judgment, according to Kant, rely on transcendentals that make our experience possible: intuitions of space and time for empirical experience of the world, the categories of understanding for explanation of experience, and categories of judgment for the moral and aesthetic dimensions of life.

Asking or insisting that something must be presupposed in order to make certain forms of experience possible is asking for an act of the imagination. For example, if as Kant argued, morality is to be a valid principle of conduct we must presuppose a will that can act contrary to inclination, then we are asked to imagine a form of behavior that seems to be restricted to the human species. Further, we are to imagine human beings capable of becoming legislators of the moral law and to act in accordance with its maxims. Moral experience, therefore, presupposes that we can envision persons as in some sense ends in themselves and therefore not to be regarded as means merely; persons who can act on maxims they are willing to become moral laws for all mankind. "Might be" and "ought to be" make no sense unless the power of imagining what isn't is posited. A similar point is made by Israel Scheffler in connection with the idea of human potential:

> Human action in fact presupposes capacities that far outreach those of other animals. Foremost among such capacities is that of *symbolic representation*, in virtue of which intentions may be expressed, anticipations formulated, purposes projected, and past outcomes recalled.[9]

The imagination is not limited by the rules of logic or constraints of reality. Yet some flights of the imagination do create new realities and forthwith become subject to the criteria of empirical inquiry. Once flights of imagination became flights of aircraft, they became domesticated members of physical reality. But when imagined entities are endowed with spiritual powers; when "what might be" is converted into "what ought to be," they create a claim to ontological status, a claim that cannot be settled by empirical tests. Thus the seeds of the controversy between objectivism and relativism are sown and generate philosophical and social strife.

The perennial jousting of objectivism and relativism in academic philosophy escapes the notice, let alone the concern, of the public school. However, when this strife is manifested in the beliefs of the citizenry, it has direct influence on the public school. The effect is felt in the decisions on curriculum, modes of teaching and the administration of the system.

Not all partisans of objectivism in value theory are motivated by religious belief. Family values, for example, which have become a political slogan in our time, are supported by large numbers of what might be called secular objectivists who regard them as the basis for good citizenship. Some receive their convictions from the social class in which they were reared. For them, respectability within the class covers a whole array of value norms that are beyond criticism. Apparently the respectability criterion is found in all social strata. The *mores* of the criminal society are as immutably "right" as those of the moneyed aristocracy. In so far as the members of a social class are members of a religious denomination, there can be mutual reinforcement of the values of both groups.

Educated groups, as some surveys have shown, are more ready than others to rely on relativistic arguments for their insistence on individual rights as against the political machinery of government and what they regard as the *mores* of the "respectable" institutions. Some blame colleges and academics for this defection from middle-class values, presumably because the academic stock in trade has been controversy between orthodoxy and challengers to it. Abelard (1079–1142) became famous for basing his teaching on it in Paris.[10]

The effect of this strife on the curriculum is too familiar to need detailed discussion. Sooner or later the question of who is to decide what is to be taught has to be faced by recognizing a distinction between political and non-political issues in education. A political issue is determined by plebiscites. Non-political ones having to do with knowledge derive their authority from the consensus of the learned. *What* is "good" history or chemistry is not a political question; *whether* history should be taught in a public school is. Whether in a democratic society the will of the majority can ever be challenged is a question that continues to concern legislators and judges.

In the United States and other democratic countries, there is usually a restraint on the powers of the electorate. A constitution may limit such powers by bills of rights and legal stipulations. Yet in the long run even such restraints can be overthrown by the will of the people, either by their votes or by revolutions that, if successful, become legitimated as formal expression of the public will. It is not enough for the school to declare its adherence to non-political authority; there must be enough understanding in the community to accept the distinction. An *educated* democratic society can be expected to do so because the citizens are familiar with both types of authority; an uneducated public may not be.

The problem-solving strand of the curriculum is one way of coping with the impasse. While the symbolics of information, basic scientific concepts, developmental strands, and exemplars are clearly committed to the authority of the consensus of the learned, the problem-solving exercise deliberately probes molar social problems for divergent views and their consequences. It would be unrealistic to expect this separation of political and non-political modes of study to be as clear-cut as one would wish. For one thing, the formal studies in the other strands are already value laden. Some creationist devotees, for example, argue that the sciences, especially those dealing with evolution, are prejudiced against religious truth. Other creationists, however, hold that evolution not creationism is bad science.[11] The developmental strands, of course, are histories of conflicting beliefs and values. Furthermore, the attempt to conduct the molar problem-solving exercises according to the rules of the CAT, much as a baseball or tennis match are governed by their respective rules, will itself arouse objections from those who regard even raising certain problems as violations of their convictions.

Despite the difficulties, this strife of values is precisely what the citizens are expected to adjudicate and what education is supposed to help them do so intelligently. This brings up once more the difficulties the citizen has in arriving at an intelligent decision. Education, of course, can help. For example, since the citizens depend so much on the media, judging their credibility is one of their major tasks. What makes one newspaper more credible than another; one magazine, one television program more reliable than another? What does the citizen know about the political and economic philosophy of the publication? Can the citizen construe the contents of the media with the interpretive resources of what has been called here the educated mind? Can the citizen make judgments of consistency or detect evidence of bias?

The citizen cannot be privy to all the circumstances that govern the media or the events they report. Even with large corps of specialists, the media are far from knowing, let alone reporting, all the facts. Even-handed reporting, on the contrary, does not facilitate the decision-making process. Sooner or later the citizen may have to act: buy or sell a stock, make a contribution to a cause, and above all vote in an election.

At this stage, after personal advantage, probable consequences, social and personal loyalties have been evaluated, there remains to be considered the criterion or principle or the system of value norms to which the citizen subscribes explicitly or implicitly. Does an act or policy of person or institution exemplify the principles to which he/she is deeply committed? Does it conform to its own declared principles? A decision by a person who does not stand to profit from it is more credible than one that does benefit the person making it. A politician arguing for a certain economic policy loses some credibility when it becomes known that his devotion is not to the wisdom of the policy but to the interests of his backers. The questions: *Cui bono*? (whose benefit) and whose ox is being gored become principles of credibility.

Life styles, styles of speech and personality are among the images that contribute to the credibility of persons and the causes they represent. These are aesthetic images in that they carry their value commitments on their very appearance. Images can and often are created to deceive, because they are important factors in credibility and action. Images persuade directly — not by argument.

Criteria of the good society

It would be difficult to envision exercises in molar problem solving that would not encounter early in the game controversies about the criteria of the good society. Even if there is consensus that the democratic society is to be preferred to others — and the common rhetoric in the United States takes for granted that it is — there is no agreement as to what "democratic" should mean. The United States, fortunately, possesses documents such as the Declaration of Independence and a Constitution that are supposed to define a democratic society, albeit a judiciary numbered in the hundreds, if not thousands, is kept busy determining what these documents really mean.

The American Creed

As Gunnar Myrdal noted, the American Creed is an amalgam of British common law, certain principles of Christianity, and of the political philosophers of the Enlightenment. He pointed out that all political parties had recourse to the Creed for justification of their policies. Rich and poor, liberals and conservatives invoked it, and the heroes of American history have been reformers in the name of the American Creed. That legal and community practice often side-stepped this ideology did not diminish its role as a creed.[12] In other words, it served as a criterion and redemptive slogan.

Myrdal regarded the principles of the Creed as high-level evaluations and when specific legislation did not conform to them, the inconsistency troubled the public. The strain to consistency, he felt, provided a principle of social criticism and reform.

The mixed composition of the Creed and the tendency to overlook its internal diversity may be the result of bringing together three heterogeneous principles: (1) the principle of achievement or the opportunity for achievement, (2) the principle of justice, and (3) the principle of compassion.[13]

Achievement, justice, compassion

The principle of achievement holds that the good society maximizes the opportunity for each individual to develop talent and energy to its highest potential. This theme runs through all the ideological documents that make up the Creed. Its application ranges from freedom of expression to freedom of economic enterprise. In a good society realizing one's potential is free from constraints, especially constraints by government.

The principle of justice, however, puts bounds on achievement, both by individuals and institutions. Free enterprise, yes; unrestricted free enterprise, no. Freedom for research, yes; unrestricted freedom, no. What limits so fundamental a principle as achievement — the admitted source of human progress in every dimension of life? The other two principles — justice and compassion — do. Justice and achievement are limited by compassion, which, in turn, faces limits by the need for achievement and the demand for fairness.

1 What is the origin of such notions as achievement, justice, or compassion? Attributing their origin to religious systems, metaphysical systems, or some unidentified nature of things is unsatisfactory to those who regard such sources as unwarranted suppositions, unwarranted, that is, on positivistic criteria. A more scientific source would be physical nature itself. For example, the urge to achievement could be derived from the struggle for survival in the animal kingdom. Survival goes to individuals of the species who are strong, energetic, or cunning enough to insure numerous progeny. The good of the species depends on achievement, and in nature this achievement has its own palpable rewards. One can, therefore, make a plausible case for regarding achievement potential as a prime criterion for a good society. However, even on this naturalistic criterion human imagination and intelligence cast doubts. The spectacle of power is always impressive and in its raw forms easily recognized and evaluated. What happens when through the power of imagination ideas of power are created that have little to do with physical power? When symbols of power, e.g., money, display, reputation, may or may not have existential denotation? In a complex society achievement itself has to be examined for genuineness. However, achievement, when genuine, is a genuine criterion of the good society.

2 Whence comes the notion of justice or fairness, if it has no counterpart in the natural selection scenario? In that scenario, the question: "Is it fair for the fox to eat the rabbit?" makes no sense, and neither the fox nor the rabbit raises the issue. Animal lovers are rebuked when they try to protect certain species from predators because they are interfering with the life chain of nature. Too few wolves make for too many elk, and too many elk means more elk will die of starvation. If the human species is like other participants in the battle for survival, what is the point of raising the issue of fairness

when the strong "naturally" win the race and reap the rewards? The point may be that the image of unfairness is literally not fair to behold and therefore repugnant on its own account. It is no accident that in trying to portray justice the image of the scale is so prominent, for scales measure balance, and balance is a basic formal property of aesthetic images.

In human affairs fairness or justice takes the form of a balance between effort and reward. A race among contestants of different speed is fair, if the winner really has superior speed and if the other contestants have not been hindered by factors having nothing to do with running ability. That the race should not go to the swift is both aesthetically and morally unacceptable. It would be unfair to trip one of the contestants, and it would be unfair to match runners who are very tall with those that are unusually short, etc. If the race is taken as an allegory for the achievement principle, it is fair that the race go to the swift, but suppose that at the end of the race the fleetest runners eliminate the late finishers? Or suppose that the winners of the first race are given head starts in subsequent races? Would that be fair? One might argue that winning the first race entitled the winner to make more sure of winning subsequent ones, as one might argue that parents having acquired great wealth by their ability and industry are entitled to give their offspring a better start in life. Would this argument qualify as being fair? One doubts it, for it runs counter to the phenomenology of fairness.

This phenomenology may have played a part in the Biblical Jubilee, according to which every fiftieth year all lands were to be returned to the tribes that originally owned them, and all Hebrew slaves were to be emancipated. For the ability to achieve not being equally distributed, it was fairly certain that in a half century the most enterprising tribes would be in possession of most of the land. To restore the balance, measures had to be invoked to insure fairness or justice.

3 The principle of compassion seems to be independent of both achievement and justice. If individuals have failed to achieve and no injustice has caused the failure, why are they entitled to sympathy? To many, compassion is a form of pity, a symbolic co-suffering. The distance between the human and animal world with respect to compassion is so remarkable as to invite the term "unnatural". There must be unlucky young sheep so that wolves may survive, and there must be wolves else the elk outrun the food supply.

Of the three principles of the good society, two run counter to Darwinian natural selection. We must conclude that justice and compassion are either unnatural or consonant only with another kind of nature, namely, human nature. Apparently there is a part of human nature that judges human conduct and desert on principles different from natural selection. Part of this human nature is the ability to imagine that matters could be otherwise — more fair, more compassionate — the notion that to be human constitutes ground for claims on others to respect that humanity. These images of the human essence may be aesthetic in origin stemming from the tendency to perceive experience as having sensory, formal, and properties expressive of moods, dynamic states, ideas and ideals. This may be straining the resources of aesthetic imagery unduly, but what other sources validate them? If the metaphysical theories of non-physical being are rejected; if religious doctrine is rejected; if natural selection is rejected, what sort of entity or process could justify the principles of the good society? Aesthetic experience mediates between the physiology of sensation and the transcendence of cognition *via* the imagination. What Susanne Langer called the "forms of feeling"[14] may be root experiences that provide the criteria for achievement, justice, and compassion. That is why the educated imagination is a necessary partner to the educated mind.

Imagery and credibility

This notion adds plausibility to the role of the aesthetic experience in judgments of credibility. To be credible, an institution, an individual, or a political theory needs to conform to a model appearance. They must present an appearance expressive of the properties they claim or are assumed to possess. This is an old story in merchandizing and advertising; that appearances may be deceiving is as old as the story, but the citizen has little else on which to judge many of the proposals and schemes on which he is expected to make intelligent judgments.

The citizen, therefore, must enlist cognitive resources to test the claims of appearances. Either the citizen has to become a specialist — one who can use formal studies for application to existential problems — or do the next best thing, viz., use the resources of schooling interpretively. This means ability to identify the issues, judge the disciplinary resources relevant to it, weigh the opinions of those who put forward solutions, and judge their consequences. These procedures are precisely what the molar problem-solving exercises do when the other components of the curriculum have stocked the allusionary base.

The potency of the aesthetic image to persuade may have its explanation in its properties. If the image is to be interesting to perceive by virtue of its appearance to the senses, then, as has been argued in previous chapters, its sensory and formal properties must combine to become expressive of a mood, a dynamic state of some sort, or an idea or ideal. If an object or an action by its appearance does not express the import it claims, it loses its credibility. It then requires other evidence to restore it.

It is not surprising, therefore, that consistency is a prime measure of sincerity. When a highly placed business executive appears on television to announce that, "We must cut wages drastically to be competitive," the public relations department would be well advised to announce that the speaker's salary would also be drastically reduced. The same advice is suitable for those who arrive at a meeting in limousines to castigate the government for neglect of the poor and homeless. The incongruence is perceived and judged immediately, i.e., without complicated chains of inference. The endorsement of liberal causes by well-to-do radical chic may be sincere but is not convincing. Neither are the protests of the "wretched poor," if their wretchedness is perceived (not inferred) as shiftlessness.

Thus logical and psychological components meld into aesthetic images, which may or may not furnish grounds for warranted assertion, but are taken into account in warranted commitment. Aesthetic images may be simple or subtle, straightforward or ambiguous. Sarcasm, irony, satire are indirect forms of communication that require appropriate sensitivity to achieve their effect.

Alexander Woollcott is reported to have apologized to a friend that his letter was so long because he did not have time to write a short one. A writer who received a lengthy criticism of his book from a reviewer might reply, "I am sure that had you more time to write this review, it would have been much shorter." The use of such apparent self-contradiction makes no sense logically. Without the interpretive resources of the reader to supply not only sense but a highly subtle juxtaposition of concepts, it makes no sense at all. Did the retort to the critic assume that the critic would be familiar with the Woollcott quip? Very probably, for these are examples of a sophisticated use of the language by persons who know their way around in the literary world.

The citizen's difficulty in interpreting problems on which decisions are to be made logically and scientifically cannot be overemphasized. We live in a society the workings of which are rarely amenable to problem solving by the Complete Act of Thought, used individually or in groups. Banking, for example, is no longer an easily construed process of making deposits and withdrawals with the understanding that the bank would take good care of the funds in the interim. That banks make loans, charge and pay interest, etc., complicates matters somewhat, but not beyond the ability of the ordinary citizen to comprehend. Nor do occasional defaults and chicanery outrun the citizen's powers of understanding. But when a huge bank located in one of the most imposing buildings in the city, with thousands of employees and machines clattering away, declares bankruptcy, the citizen is confounded, for two sorts of reasons. First is the aesthetic incongruity of an image of invincible power and reliability in the process of disintegration. Second is the explanation of the failure, viz., that the bank made bad loans to firms in foreign countries; that it had loaned huge amounts to venture capitalists, who, in turn, tried to take control of huge corporations, which had invested in enterprises that were now heavily in debt, etc., etc., etc. The citizen, with a high school and college diploma, is lost in the maze of economics, politics, and, above all, modern technology. It not only passes understanding but shocks the images of reliability and solidity that grounded belief.

Cognitive and evaluative maps

How can the citizen judge measures proposed or opposed to the regulation of the banking industry? Adequate qualifications for making intelligent decisions might be the ability to read the *Wall Street Journal* from stock quotations to editorials, to specialized essays. It would also require the citizen to distinguish carefully between the reports of financial happenings in that *Journal* and its editorial policy. The interpretation of the same set of facts and reports by the *New York Times*, the *Washington Post*, and the *Wall Street Journal* will vary considerably. Can the citizen dig into shelves of specialized financial reports to help make up his or her mind? These are fairly unrealistic expectations, so the citizen relies on judgments by experts and commentators on television who, unfortunately, disagree on virtually all issues. Does confidence in the Prudential financial enterprises rest on reading balance sheets or on its trademark, the Rock of Gibraltar?

Reliance on images is risky, albeit they play an important role in judgment, but how is the citizen to use information if it is complicated beyond reasonably educated powers of understanding? A plausible answer lies in the associative and interpretive uses of general education. The associative resources include mixtures of cognitive and psychological contents, habits gleaned from many sources, as well as images and ideas from school experience. Some of these studies will have the power to enrich and clarify experience. The studies of the sciences, developmental studies, and the exemplars should provide cognitive and evaluative maps on which the problems of the citizen can be located and their relations discerned. Educated associative and interpretive resources together should provide the citizen with enlightened conjectures.

Of the two kinds of maps, the cognitive are less controversial, because they derive from disciplines in which the consensus of the learned is far better established than in those dealing with values. The exemplar segment of the curriculum introduces the student to a kind of consensus that is validated by both scholarship and connoisseurship. The exemplars *display* as well as *argue* their claims to excellence. If their images and ideas are introjected so that they become vectors in the perceiver's own taste, that taste can be called an *educated* taste. Despite the dictum: *de gustibus non disputandum*, one can properly speak of an "educated" taste. A taste determined by study of exemplars could so qualify, because the exemplars by definition are works that scholars have recognized as embodying the values of a particular period or style, or as illustrating transitions between periods, or works that were "ahead" of their own time. Thus some early abstract works of art are now regarded as exemplars because they were "ahead of their time." However, had their time not come, they would be regarded as oddities rather than exemplars. Whether a particular work deserves the exemplar status constitutes the subject matter of scholarly criticism.

Two major objections to this view of the role of education in the field of values, especially the role here given to exemplars, are (1) that exemplars are given a superior status they do not deserve in a world where all values are taken to be relative to social, psychological, and political factors, and (2) their indoctrination by the school is indefensible on both intellectual and moral grounds.

The response to the first objection is perhaps on the churlish side, because the argument against an objective theory of value can be invoked against the claim of universal relativity of values as well. There is conclusive *empirical* evidence for neither. The objectivist view is supported by the *fact* that value systems have become embodied in exemplars, not only in the arts, but in institutions and cultures as well. That different institutions and cultures do not embody the same values does not imply that they are not embodied in exemplars.

As to the propriety of allowing a selected set of exemplars to influence a generation of school children, one can only point out that neither children nor adults can escape the impact of images that have become exemplars of some value system. To teach exemplars while in the same breath warning pupils not to be influenced by them will strike even the most modest intellect as a stultifying enterprise.

Whether the *Iliad* or *The Divine Comedy* or Picasso's *Guernica* will capture the imagination is not guaranteed by their inclusion in the curriculum or excluded by warnings of relativity. Once the exemplars have been experienced, their persuasiveness is no longer a matter of calculated choice. They either capture the imagination or they do not. Whether the capture is permanent or not depends on what subsequent experience does to what has been learned in school. To give schooling power to determine this in advance is presumptuous indeed. Whatever honorific connotation one confers on the term "education" does not automatically adhere to schooling. School cannot hope to anticipate the social, economic, and political factors that shape or distort the patterns of life. That is why the best the school can do is to validate its choice of exemplars by scholarship. On this there can be disciplined debate among scholars, but the debate need not be replicated in the curriculum, at least not in the curriculum of the elementary and secondary school. It is a debate that curriculum theorists should take seriously for it contains the reasons and arguments by which their choices of curriculum content are defended.

The exemplars do portray value norms that enable the learner to distinguish existential alternatives and their often conflicting claims. Which alternatives will be chosen in the life of the citizen the school cannot foretell, but the school cannot be faulted for not exposing the pupil to notable exemplars of possibility.

In the end, exemplars like the sciences, development studies, and molar problem solving can do no more than to enrich the allusionary base with their imagic and cognitive resources. The schools can only hope that tacitly these studies will convey intimations of importance, perhaps of ultimate importance.

Notes

Introduction: Proper claims and expectations
1 Center for Statistics, US Department of Education.
2 Herbert I. London, "Liberal Arts: Learning from Past Mistakes," *Wall Street Journal*, August, 11, 1986.

Chapter 1 Criteria for uses of schooling
1 For a full discussion of the subject, see D. L. Clark, *Rhetoric in Greco-Roman Education*, New York, Columbia University Press, 1957. See also references to "memorization" in H. S. Broudy and John R. Palmer, *Exemplars of Teaching Method*, Chicago, Rand McNally, 1965.
2 *Politics*, 1337^{a}11–1338^{b}4.
3 In a project involving a study of engineering education at a large research university, it was thought desirable for engineers to hear how professors in other fields carried on their work. A well-known classicist was invited to describe his work, and he recited his research in the bibliography of a certain period and how he was utilizing the latest electronic devices for analyzing the data. He described his daily schedule of teaching graduate courses, the journals to which he contributed, and the book on which he was working. To which the listening engineers remarked that the classicist seemed to do the sort of things that they themselves did, and that they saw nothing especially humanistic about it.
4 I have been struck by the biologist Garrett Hardin's observations that when an internal human function such as walking or doing mental arithmetic is externalized into a machine, the organism has to find a substitute organic activity to preserve the powers it embodied or suffer its atrophy. "An Evolutionist Looks at Computers," *DATAMATION*, May, 1969. For a more extended discussion of this topic, cf. my chapter on technology and citizenship in *Microcomputers and Education*, 85th Yearbook of the National Society for the Study of Education, 1986, pp. 234–53.
5 Cf. my "The Humanities and their Uses: Proper Claims and Expectation," *Journal of Aesthetic Education*, vol. 17, no. 4, pp. 126–38.
6 I have tested this with college students and found that the association

with rubber heels was not obvious, whereas to some of my academic colleagues it was too obvious to be interesting. For some students the reference to Achilles did not ring the right bell; for others the word "rubber" did not arouse the expected association, perhaps because rubber heels are not advertised as frequently as they once were.

7 Grover Smith devoted 26 pages, in his *T. S. Eliot's Poetry and Plays*, University of Chicago Press, 1950, to the sources of meaning of the beginning section of *The Waste Land* called "The Burial of the Dead."

8 Martin Gardner, "WAP, SAP, PAP, & FAP," *New York Review of Books*, May 8, 1986, vol. 33, no. 38, p. 23.

9 Cf. R. H. Ennis, "Critical Thinking and the Curriculum," *National Forum*, vol. 65, Winter, 1986.

Chapter 2   General Education – proper claims and expectations

1 *Plato's Protagoras*, ed. by Gregory Vlastos, New York, The Liberal Arts Press, 1956.

2 Werner Jaeger, *Paideia: The Ideals of Greek Culture*, trans. by Gilbert Highet, New York, Oxford University Press, 1943–5.

3 Cf. H. S. Broudy, "Three Modes of Teaching and Their Evaluation," in *Evaluation of Teaching*, Bloomington, Ind., *Phi Delta Kappa*, 1975, pp. 5–11. Also my "Didactics, Heuristics, and Philetics," *Educational Theory*, vol. 22, no. 3, 1972, pp. 251–61.

4 *Feeling and Form*, New York, Scribner's, 1953, and *Philosophy in a New Key*, Cambridge, Mass, Harvard University Press, 1942.

5 H. S. Broudy and John Palmer, *Exemplars of Teaching Method*, Chicago, Rand McNally, 1965, pp. 95 ff.

6 Samuel Taylor Coleridge, *Biographia Literaria*, J. Shawcross, ed., Oxford University Press, 1907.

7 For a detailed treatment of this point, cf. C. DeDeugd, *The Significance of Spinoza's First Kind of Knowledge*, Utrecht, Van Gorcum, 1966, pp. 72–3.

8 Quoted from President Ronald Reagan's State of the Union Message, January 1986.

9 "Of Cerebrums and Computer Chips," *University of Rochester Research Review*, describing the research of Dana Ballard, Spring, 1986, pp. 6–7.

10 *Economic Education in the Schools*, Committee for Economic Development, New York, The Committee, 1961.

11 Thomas S. Kuhn, *The Structure of Scientific Revolutions,* University of Chicago Press, 1962, p. 11.

12 Translated by Richard Howard and published by Hill & Wang, *New York Review of Books*, vol. 33, no. 8, May 8, 1986, p. 44.

Chapter 3   The search for evidence

1 *The Basic Works of Cicero*, Moses Hadas, ed., New York, Random House, 1951, p. 176.

2 *Ibid.*, p. 179.
3 The selections, responses, and interviews can be found in the Report on Case Studies on the Uses of Knowledge to the Spencer Foundation, ERIC, 224–315.
4 *Sylvia Plath Collected Poems*, edited by Ted Hughes, Boston, Faber & Faber, 1981, p. 139.
5 Case Studies Report, p. 110.

Chapter 4   Tacit knowing or knowing with

1 According to Cyril Burt, G. F. Stout was the first to set forth the account of this type of knowing clearly in his *Analytic Psychology*, 1896, Bk 1, Chapter 4, and it had been discussed even earlier by George Berkeley, R. H. Lotze, and Edmund Burke, "Personal Knowledge, Art, and the Humanities," *Journal of Aesthetic Education*, vol. 3, no. 2, 1969, 29–47. Cf. my "On Knowing With," *Proceedings of the Philosophy of Education Society*, 1979, and responses by Martin Levit and Philip G. Smith, pp. 89–116.
2, 1969, 29–47. Cf. my "On Knowing With," *Proceedings of the Excellence in American Secondary Education*, Chicago, Rand McNally, 1964.
3 Michael Polanyi, *The Tacit Dimension*, New York, Doubleday, 1966.
4 H. S. Broudy, *Truth and Credibility: The Citizen's Dilemma*, New York, Longman's, 1981.
5 Alexander Nehamas, reviewing *The Idea of the Good in Platonic-Aristotelian Philosophy*, trans. by P. Christopher Smith, New Haven, Yale University Press, 1986, in *The New York Times Book Review*, June 15, 1986, p.29.
6 Gilbert Ryle, *The Concept of Mind*, London, Hutchinson, 1949.
7 *Einfühlung* or the projection of one's feelings into the object contemplated is frequently encountered in aesthetic theory, for example, Vernon Lee's explanation of the mountain rises. Vernon Lee and C. Anstruther-Thomson, *Beauty and Ugliness and Other Studies in Psychological Aesthetics*, London, John Lane, 1912.
8 Portions of this discussion were incorporated in "The Uses of Schooling in Professional Life," *Tradition and Discovery: the Polanyi Society Periodical*, vol. 13, no. 2, Spring 1985.
9 E. Ripple and V. N. Rockdaele, eds, *Piaget Rediscovered*, Ithaca, NY, School of Education, Cornell University, 1964, p. 19.
10 H. A. Ayer, *Language, Truth and Logic*, London, Oxford University Press, 1936, pp. 18–19.
11 "Sense Giving and Sense Reading" in *Knowing and Being*. Essays by Michael Polanyi. ed. Marjorie Grene, University of Chicago Press, 1969, pp. 180–1.
12 Cf. Polanyi's "The Creative Imagination," *Chemical Engineering News*,

44, 1968, 27–43, and "The Unaccountable Element in Science," in *Knowing and Being, op. cit.*

13 In this connection it is interesting to consider the hypothesis about transfer put forward by Gertrude Hendrix in her article, "A New Clue to Transfer of Training," *Elementary School Journal*, vol. 48, no. 4, 1947, p. 198. She finds that for generalizing of transfer power, the unverbalized awareness method of learning is better than a method in which an authoritative statement of the generalization comes first, and that verbalizing a generalization immediately after discovery may actually decrease transfer power.

14 Cf. for detailed discussion of these ideas, Polanyi's *Personal Knowledge*, University of Chicago Press, 1958; *Science, Faith and Society*, University of Chicago Press, 1946; *The Tacit Dimension*, New York, Doubleday, 1966; Anchor Books, 1967. For a thorough treatment of Polanyi's theory of knowledge, see Marjorie Grene, *The Knower and the Known*, New York, Basic Books, 1966.

Chapter 5   The role of imagery in uses of schooling

1 A description of the project and its implementation by the teachers who participated is to be found in *The Aesthetic Eye: Teacher-to-Teacher Talk*, edited by Frances D. Hine, Gilbert A. Clark, W. Dwaine Greer, and Ronald A. Silverman, Los Angeles County Superintendent of Schools, 1977.

2 These properties were organized into a diagram called "The Nature of Informed Aesthetic Response," with the help of Ronald Silverman of the California State College at Los Angeles. See Figure 6.2, page 84–5.

3 "Relativism, Power, and Philosophy," Presidential Address, Eastern Division of the American Philosophical Association, December 29, 1984.

4 Fred Dretske, Presidential Address, *Proceedings of the Western Division of the American Philosophical Association*, April 26, 1985, pp. 23–4.

5 *The Divorce Between the Sciences and the Humanities*, Second Tykociner Lecture, University of Illinois, 1975, pp. 23–4.

6 C. Fries, *American English Grammar*, New York, D. Appleton Century, 1940, p. 288.

7 William Bulter Yeats, *Collected Poems*, New York, Macmillan Co., 1956, p. 191.

8 H. S. Broudy and John Palmer, *Exemplars of Teaching Method*, Chicago, Rand McNally, 1965, Chapter 2 *et passim.*

9 By serious or academic art is here meant art that has become a target of scholarship, the concern of art historians and critics and other components of the art world. Thus a popular art, such as jazz, has become an academic art on which research, study, and university degrees are conferred. It has become serious art.

10 Foster Wygant, *Art in American Schools in the Nineteenth Century,* Cincinnati, Interwood Press, 1983, reviewed by Margaret DiBlasio in the *Journal of Aesthetic Education,* vol. 20, no. 2, 1986, 109–11.

11 The notion of a discipline-based curriculum in art education was outlined by W. Dwaine Greer, "A Discipline-Based View of Art Education," *Studies in Art Education,* vol. 22, no. 4, 1984, 217–18. Cf. W. D. Greer and J. C. Rush, "A Grand Experiment: the Getty Institute for Educators in the Visual Arts," *Art Education,* vol. 35, no. 24, 1985, 33–5. Cf. Ralph A. Smith, *Excellence in Art Education,* NAEA, Reston, Va., 1986.

12 It should be noted that, although the discussion has seemed to concentrate on visual art, aesthetic scanning is applicable to any of the media, music, dance, literature, and drama. The development of the property systems in these media would do much to promote formal study of these arts – as arts – in general education.

Chapter 6   The curriculum and the uses of schooling.

1 The design for this analysis was prepared by Professor Ronald H. Silverman and the author for a project called *The Aesthetic Eye* described in the previous chapter. A more recent description of the project is available in Ann Bachtel-Nash, "Teaching Aesthetic Perception in the Elementary School," *Art Education,* September 1985.

2 *Ibid.,* p. 6.

3 Terms coined by Joseph T. Tykociner, *Research as a Science–Zetetics,* Urbana, Electrical Engineering Research Laboratory, University of Illinois, 1959, pp. 30–3.

4 "Our analysis indicates that it is clearly not the school subject called history that enables us to understand the past, but science – economics, anthropology, psychology, and the other sciences," John R. Palmer, "The place of History in the Curriculum," *School Review,* vol. 71, no. 2, Summer 1963, p. 214.

Chapter 7   The citizen's use of schooling

1 *Democracy and Education,* New York, Macmillan, 1916.

2 *Teachers' College Record,* 1918, 319–35.

3 *Ethics and the Limits of Philosophy,* Cambridge, Mass., Harvard University Press, 1986.

4 For a view that seems to equate all education with group inquiry, see Herbert A. Thelen, *Education and the Human Quest,* New York, Harper, 1960.

5 This was specifically addressed in a volume by some adherents of the Dewey approach to epistemology and schooling who felt that it did not stress sufficiently these psychological factors in the Complete Act of Thought. R. Bruce Raup, Kenneth Benne, George E. Axtelle, and B.

Othanel Smith, *The Improvement of Practical Intelligence*, New York, Harper, 1950.

6 Cf. James J. Shields and Colin Greer, eds, *Foundations of Education: Dissenting Views*, New York, John Wiley, 1974.

7 Among these books were Allen Graubard, *Free the Children*, New York, Pantheon Books, 1972; John Holt, *Freedom and Beyond*, New York, Dutton, 1972; Ivan Illich, *Deschooling Society*, New York, Harper & Row, 1971; Jonathan Kozol, *Free Schools*, Boston, Houghton Mifflin, 1972; A. S. Neill, *Summerhill*, New York, Hart, 1960; Paul Goodman, *Compulsory Miseducation*, New York, Horizon Press, 1964; Neil Postman and Charles Weingartner, *Teaching as a Subversive Activity*, New York, Dell Publishing Co., Delacorte Press,1969; Samuel Bowles and Herbert Gintis, *Schooling in Capitalist America*, Beverly Hills, CA, Sage, 1977; Paulo Freire, *Pedagogy of the Oppressed*, 1973, *Education for Critical Consciousness*, 1977, and *Pedagogy in Process*, 1978 – all New York, Seabury Press; Pierre Bourdieu and Jean-Claude Passeron, *Reproduction in Education, Society and Culture*, Beverly Hills, CA, Sage, 1977; Basil Bernstein, *Class, Codes and Control*, vol. 3, London, Routledge & Kegan Paul, 1977; Martin Carnoy and Henry M. Levin, *The Limits of Educational Reform*, New York, David McKay and Co., Inc., 1976; Michel Foucault, *The Archeology of Knowledge and the Discourse of Language*, New York, Harper & Row, 1972; Michael Katz, *Class, Bureaucracy, and Schools: The Illusion of Educational Change in America*, New York, Praeger, 1975; Clarence J. Karier, *The Shaping of the American Educational State*, New York, Free Press, 1975; Jurgen Habermas, *Knowledge and Human Interests*, trans, Jeremy J. Shapiro, Boston, Beacon Press, 1971; Michael Apple, *Ideology and Curriculum*, London, Routledge & Kegan Paul, 1979; Michael Harrington, *The Twilight of Capitalism*, New York, Simon & Schuster, 1976; George Lukács, *History and Class Consciousness*, trans. Rodney Livingstone, Cambridge, Mass., MIT Press, 1971; and Antonio Gramsci, *Prison Notebooks*, trans. Quintin Hoare and Geoffrey Nowell Smith, New York, International Publishers, 1971.

8 A number of essays on this topic are to be found in Douglas Sloan, ed., *Education and Values*, New York, Teachers College, 1980; Israel Scheffler, *Of Human Potential*, London, Routledge & Kegan Paul, 1985; and Brian Crittenden, *Cultural Pluralism and Common Curriculum*, Carlton, Victoria, Melbourne University Press, 1982.

9 *Of Human Potential, op. cit.,* p. 17.

10 In his *Sic et Non*, Abelard formulated 158 questions about the Trinity, Redemption, and the Sacraments. In one column he placed "Yes" answers of the authorities, and in an opposite column the "No" answers. How were these "contradictions" to be reconciled? This became the style of his teaching. Cf. H. S. Broudy and John R. Palmer,

Exemplars of Teaching Method, Chicago, Rand McNally, 1965.

11 Stephen Jay Gould scrutinizes this and kindred issues in reviewing recent books on sociobiology, "Cardboard Darwinism," *New York Review of Books*, vol. 33, no. 14, September 25, 1986, pp. 47 ff.

12 *An American Dilemma,* New York, Harper 1944.

13 For a detailed discussion of these norms, cf. my "Criteria for a Humane Society," *Educational Studies*, vol. 8, no. 1, 1977, 37–51. See also John Rawls, *A Theory of Justice*, Cambridge, Belknap Press, 1971.

14 *Feeling and Form*, London Routledge & Kegan Paul, 1953.

Index